# Love Deformed, Love Transformed

# Love Deformed, Love Transformed

A Christian Response to Sexual Addiction

David C. Bellusci

PICKWICK *Publications* · Eugene, Oregon

LOVE DEFORMED, LOVE TRANSFORMED
A Christian Response to Sexual Addiction

Pickwick Publications
An Imprint of Wipf and Stock Publishers
199 W. 8th Ave., Suite 3
Eugene, OR 97401

www.wipfandstock.com

PAPERBACK ISBN: 978-1-5326-7792-2
HARDCOVER ISBN: 978-1-5326-7793-9
EBOOK ISBN: 978-1-5326-7794-6

*Cataloguing-in-Publication data:*

Names: Bellusci, David C., author.

Title: Love deformed, love transformed : a Christian response to sexual addiction / David C. Bellusci.

Description: Eugene, OR: Pickwick Publications, 2019 | Includes bibliographical references and index.

Identifiers: ISBN 978-1-5326-7792-2 (paperback) | ISBN 978-1-5326-7793-9 (hardcover) | ISBN 978-1-5326-7794-6 (ebook)

Subjects: LCSH: Compulsive behavior—Religious aspects—Christianity | Recovery movement—Religious aspects—Christianity | Church work with recovering addicts | Habit breaking—Religious aspects—Christianity | Sex addiction

Classification: BV4598.7 B45 2019 (paperback) | BV4598.7 (ebook)

Manufactured in the U.S.A.                                   06/28/19

This work is dedicated to the individuals who crossed my path who helped me understand their suffering, and who desired to live chaste lives. This book would not have been possible without them.

Blessed are the pure in heart:  they shall see God (Matt 5:8)

# Contents

# Acknowledgements

I am grateful to professor Didier Caenepeel, OP who provided scholarly guidance for my research offering comments and suggestions. Professor Caenepeel's time, his patience, and his numerous readings of my manuscript served to improve the quality of this work.

In Thomistic studies I am especially grateful for the Communauté Saint Jean who introduced me to St. Thomas Aquinas, scholar and spiritual master, as well as the Aristotelian metaphysical foundation to Aquinas's thought. I am also thankful for the teachings of Father Lawrence Dewan, OP on Saint Thomas Aquinas and the *Summa Theologiae*.

Professors Michel Gourgues, OP and Walter Vogels, MAfr opened me to a deeper theological understanding of New Testament and Old Testament Scriptures, respectively. I am grateful for their scholarship and for the transmission of their research.

Professor John H. Morgan provided me with feedback in clinical pastoral psychotherapy in terms of theory, and research; I am grateful for Professor Morgan's professional and scholarly references especially in the areas of classical schools of psychotherapy.

A special thanks to Reverend Ajith Varghese my clinical mentor who helped me in the practical context of pastoral/clinical work in the hospital setting. Rev. Varghese taught me the value of listening to patients and providing empathetic support.

*Acknowledgements*

Dr. Hannah Pytlak has been a helpful listener for my own "issues"; I am grateful to Dr. Pytlak for the many days, months and years of attentiveness to me as an individual.

Sister Marie-Thérèse Nadeau, CND who passed away in the Autumn of 2018 offered years of dedicated service as Professor and Dean of Theology at the Dominican University College in Ottawa. Her presence enriched the College and my own theological formation.

# Introduction

The purpose of this book is to look at the different factors associated with sexual addiction, from possible causes to compulsive sexual patterns, and to provide a moral evaluation of sexual addiction with paths of support. The present study of sexual addiction, therefore, has as an objective to offer a moral perspective and evaluation of sexual addiction in view of spiritual counselling, but also to suggest a form of support that can be offered at a more psychological level. To determine the causes of sexual addiction, psychoanalytical research is considered, in addition to the neurobiological findings connected to addiction.

In order to reach a moral evaluation of the sex addict's actions and behavior, and to suggest avenues of support, therapeutic and spiritual, to overcoming addiction, I use a Christian/ Thomistic moral anthropology. The choice of turning to Thomas Aquinas is that, (i) he provides an approach that is both subjective and objective in his analyses of human acts connecting these two dimensions of morality; (ii) his emphasis on will in relation to habit has implications for sexual addictions; and finally, (iii) Aquinas offers a moral reflection that is theologically motivated, and which is important for the possible paths of spiritual counselling. I will show that Aquinas's anthropology provides a moral foundation and moral structure upon which a person's moral activity may be evaluated in sexual addiction. This same moral anthropology further suggests the help that is needed to overcome addictive patterns in the form of therapeutic and spiritual support. Based on the

Thomistic moral perspective, paths of care are presented. I further consider the avenues of care offered to help the addict's gradual re-integration, at the emotional, affective and spiritual levels. In my book I maintain that both therapy and spiritual counselling are needed to recover from addiction, and to progress to personal growth. The spiritual framework pre-supposes threefold relations which are at stake: (i) with the self because the individual becomes progressively fragmented due to actions they feel they are unable to control; (ii) in relation to the other since actions have consequences in relation to other individuals; and finally (iii) with God, where an increasing rupture with God creates a feeling of despair.

In chapter 1 I focus on studies in sexual addiction and I propose subsuming the signs of sexual addiction into three categories: (i) repeated acts; (ii) out of control behavior; and (iii) the consequences of addiction. Chapter 2 examines underlying factors and the neurotic manifestations of sexual addiction by looking at psychoanalysis and four types of sexual addiction.

In chapter 3 my option of a Christian moral anthropology drawing from Thomas Aquinas serves as a starting point in terms of understanding human nature, but also as a basis of the dynamics for acquiring virtue. Aquinas's moral anthropology is further oriented to an end which enables me to offer the suggestions for possible help among sex addicts.

In the first sections of chapter 3 I look at the interior principles of human nature through the tripartite division of the soul, as well as the last end. Since the role of the will is crucial in moral activity, I examine the voluntary and involuntary in relation to intelligence, the will and passions. I continue with the interior principles by considering habit and disposition since these are both relevant in addiction and overcoming the compulsive sexual condition. I also specifically address the moral problem of sin. In the remaining sections of chapter 3 I consider the external principles, the voluntarist approach to moral acts, as well as the supernatural role of grace.

Sexual addiction is about the obsessive-compulsive need to experience sexual pleasure; so, all of chapter 4 is devoted to pleasure. In this chapter I also consider the specific morality of pleasure. I look specifically at how Aquinas presents lust and its diverse manifestations.

In chapter 5, I offer some elements for a moral evaluation and suggest some paths for assistance based on both the psychoanalytical material presented, and the moral considerations. In terms of suggested care, I offer two approaches to the problem of sexual addiction; one is based primarily on psychological/therapeutic models of support especially in terms of Freudian interpretations of sexual addiction, and the other at a pastoral level.

The spiritual/pastoral care begins for the addict by recognizing the need for conversion, that without God's help, neither spiritual conversion nor moral transformation is possible. The avenues of support have as an aim emotional and spiritual healing, with the hope that the person may become more integrated, through a renewed relationship with God, the other, and the self. I show that the different paths of support should reduce the "acting out" and increase over time periods of abstinence, despite relapses that may arise. I end with the eschatological understanding of human existence. This distinctly Christian framework serves to shape moral conduct, human choices and actions, because the ultimate human finality is union with God.

# 1

# Sexual Addiction
## Meaning and Possible Causes

In this first chapter, I examine sexual addiction based on patterns associated with obsessive-compulsive sexual behavior suggestive of addiction. In order to explore the means by which a person suffering from sexual addiction can be offered help, and to provide support towards recovery, a working definition for "sexual addiction" is needed which is what I set out to do in this first chapter. The suggestive patterns of sexual addiction with the neurobiological and psychoanalytical components examined in chapter 2 will provide the basis of a moral evaluation.

## Identifying Sexual Addiction[1]

Sex is essential in the sense that it ensures the survival of the human species, humans are biologically wired for this purpose, and this is how God created humans, that they may become one, be fruitful

---

1. A distinction is made between "substance" addiction (alcohol, cocaine) and "process" addiction (gambling, eating, sex). See Poland and Graham, *Addiction and Responsibility*, 2.

and multiply.[2] Besides its procreative power, sexuality serves as the foundation for the construction of sexual identity; who we are, and our understanding and perception of ourselves, is also determined by what sex we are.[3] Furthermore, human sexuality expresses itself as a unitive and binding force.[4] Because of built-in sexual instincts and the psychosexual dynamics of sexual identity, sex is powerful as much as it can be frightening.[5] Powerful because sexual desire can seem to impose itself on an individual who feels overwhelmed by his/her own feelings of powerlessness; and frightening because a person can be moved to extremes in sexual conduct that might seem to go against a person's will.[6] In both instances, sex as powerful and sex as frightening, suggests something involuntary; the role of the will needs to be better understood in sexual activity in general and in addictive conduct in particular.[7]

The powerful and frightening character of human sexuality is due to the vulnerability of the person in their own sexuality, being perceived as an object of sexual desire. Human sexuality creates a sense of "vulnerability and exposure" because individuals feel that sexual exposure of their body parts and sexual acts to the public should be safeguarded as something private.[8] The fact that sex is powerful is evident in how sexual activity is expressed even "against" one's will, as individuals confess from their own experiences: a person who is married and enters into a committed

2. Gen 1:28.

3. Farley, *Christian Sexual Ethics*, 134–36.

4. Thevenot, *Repères Éthiques*, 18, 23.

5. Psychosexual development will be examined in the following chapter.

6. Carnes, *Don't Call it Love*, 10–11. Carnes is the clinical director for the Program of Sexual Dependency and Sexual Trauma at De Almo Hospital in Torrance, California. Also, see Richard Garett, "Addiction, Paradox, and the Good I Would," in Poland and Graham, *Addiction and Responsibility*, 25–53. A Christian anthropology to the human will is treated in chapter 3 below.

7. Although I focus on the will, I show both in this first and second chapters, the significance of psychosexual and neurobiological factors, in addition to environmental elements. My main area of concern from a moral perspective is the exercise of the will in the case of sexual addiction.

8. Bradshaw, *Healing the Shame*, 264.

monogamous relationship, suddenly enters into a sexual relationship with a second, third, fourth partners; a man or woman who engages in homosexual/lesbian sexual activity as a means of sexual experimentation are instances showing the power sexual desires have.[9] In sexual behavior and the powerful feeling in the experience of sexual pleasure also means "to make feelings of emptiness or numbness go away . . ."[10]

Addiction occurs when the repeated pursuit of the object of the sexual desire is unwanted, making the act "involuntary," not in reference to a single involuntary act but conditions in which sexual acts are repeated, making it impossible for the person to stop the sexual acts resulting in undesirable consequences.[11] Addiction, therefore, has to do with the repetition of involuntary sexual activity, and the undesirable consequences that follow.[12] Patrick Carnes gives ten signs as an indication of sexual addiction: (i) a pattern of out-of-control behavior; (ii) severe consequences due to the sexual behavior; (iii) inability to stop; (iv) pursuit of destructive or high risk behavior; (v) ongoing desire or effort to limit sexual behavior; (vi) sexual obsession and fantasy as a primary coping strategy; (vii) increasing amounts of sexual experience because the current level of activity is no longer sufficient; (viii) severe mood changes around sexual activity; (ix) inordinate amounts of time spent in obtaining sex, being sexual or recovering from sexual experience; (x) neglect of important social, occupational, or recreational activities because of sexual behavior.[13]

9. Sue Silverman's autobiography, *Love Sick*, demonstrates through a personal testimony the power of sexual addiction.

10. Longo et al., "Effects of Internet Sexuality," 93.

11. It should be made clear from the outset that I am not examining the morality of sexual acts, but rather, sexual acts that are perceived by the subject as being unmanageable because of their compulsive nature.

12. I will be examining involuntary and voluntary acts in the subsequent sections. I should point out that whether these acts are involuntary or not will also be affected by the person's psychological condition. This will be also considered throughout my work.

13. Carnes, *Don't Call it Love*, 11–12. The Jesuit psychologist and philosopher Giovanni Cucci identifies three signs, "introversion," "time consumed,"

Examining these ten signs associated with addiction more closely, problems arise with each of these ten categories suggesting that addictive signs are more complex and less categorical than they may appear to be in terms of both the psychological and moral aspects of addiction. This suggests that some reinterpreting and regrouping the signs of sexual addiction may be needed and should be considered. With the first sign, there is the difficulty as to how one determines "out-of-control" behavior; this category appears rather subjective and needs some way of objectifying the criterion of "out of control" so that it is not only a subjective evaluation, but where objective grounds can be identified for determining "out-of-control" behavior.

A case study presents out-of-control sexual behavior stemming from violence in the home, when masturbating and fantasizing violent sex in childhood that becomes a coping mechanism.[14] The violent family history transforms into addictive patterns; the presence of early childhood abuse predisposes the individual to a certain vulnerability to later addiction, the blurring of sexual partners and love. The pattern of abuse transforms into reckless sexual behavior and loss of moral parameters; the person has "lost control," exacerbating the situation with drugs and alcohol. Interrelational behavior shows a rupture with reality, especially, the failure to pursue an objective good for oneself or for others.

One of the elements of sexual addiction where it differs from substance abuse is that a person's body is instrumentalized from "within" as a tool used to create pleasure, while drugs and alcohol create pleasure introduced from the outside.[15] By instrumentalizing the body, pleasure has a form of escape, a pain-killer, and functions the way drugs and alcohol are used to bring pleasure to the body.[16] The high that is experienced with an orgasm leads ad-

---

and "out of control" (*Dipendenza Sessuale Online*, 13).

14. Carnes, *Don't Call it Love*, 12.

15. Poland and Graham, *Addiction and Responsibility*, 2.

16. Milkman and Sunderwirth show in their work summarizing the neurochemistry of sexuality that "the relationship between endorphins and orgasms was demonstrated by a group of neuroscientists who showed that the level of

dicts to compare the sexual climax of intercourse to cocaine.[17] In her novel based on her recovery from sexual addiction, Sue Silverman writes in a scene, "So, I can't leave here. I need Rick. One last time. One last high. One last fix."[18] Silverman uses the language of alcohol and drugs to describe her condition, needing sex/having sex, is compared to a "fix." While certain environmental factors may pre-dispose the individual to sexual addiction, the prevailing question is why some individuals would become sex addicts, and others, would not, instead, becoming different kind of addicts, whether it is drug or alcohol abuse. In this first sign of addiction, family environment/history is considered as a contributing factor.

In the second category relating to "severe consequences" such a claim can be true for any kind of moral conduct that is interpreted as unacceptable or inappropriate, it does not only limit itself to addictive sexual behavior. Yet, if the consequences are identified as "severe" it is because they are specifically the result of the sexual activity, and such severe outcomes connected to sexual activity include AIDS, STDs, abortion, as well as the results of the sexual misconduct ranging from job loss, marital break-up to arrests.[19] This high-risk behavior reflects the "it doesn't matter" attitude. Sexual addiction as high-risk behavior is really no different than substance abuse where a person puts their life in jeopardy because of the very nature of addictive patterns of needs that are powerful and uncontrollable. Sexual addiction does not necessarily have a relational component if it is limited to pornography, masturbation and cybersex (where there is no physical contact with another person).

The "inability to stop," the third category, may seem as if the person has no will power whatsoever. Psychological factors need

---

endorphins in the blood of hamster increased dramatically after several ejaculations" (*Craving for Ecstasy*, 45).

17. Neurobiological aspects will be discussed in the next chapter.

18. Silverman, *Love Sick*, 14

19. Because the consequences of sexual addiction cannot be verified scientifically as one finds with alcohol and drug addiction, and because sex is an integral part of the human being, not all psychologists agree whether sexual addiction is actually an addiction (see next chapter).

to be considered in this category; the person may not be able to put an end to the activities because of a high degree of fulfillment at a psychological level and not just at the sexual one—there may very well be a response to psychosexual needs. The case of marriage perceived as a solution to the excessive sexual activity before marriage, when, instead, marriage exacerbates the sexual compulsion because the addict has now entered a life-time commitment in a monogamous relationship.[20] With marital sexual intercourse being inadequate (twice a day), the addict satisfies the unfulfilled sexual needs through masturbation. Later, sexual encounters with prostitutes and homosexuals become part of the routine sexual experience in addition to the existing marital sex and masturbation. The consequences in this case would also be financial (no longer just psychological and moral) because of the costs involved paying for female and male prostitutes, and their drug habits. In sexual activity, one may be responding to emotional needs that were never fulfilled, as Silverman states, "I don't do this [daily sex with a married man in a motel] for pleasure, I do this for love."[21]

"High risk behavior," the fourth category, is another psychological category which is treated as self-destructive behavior. High-risk or self-destructive behavior does not mean, of course, addiction. Determining at which stage the behavior is an addictive one in relation to high-risk or self-destructive remains unclear. Sexual behavior may be high-risk without being addictive, as in engaging in casual sex with prostitutes. On the other hand, sexual experiences may be frequent, whether its daily masturbation or viewing pornography, or changing sexual partners, it still does not mean the behavior is addictive or even high-risk. Pursuit of sexual behavior that is self-destructive because of its consequences may not be the result of addiction but a lifestyle choice, and so the underlying psychological factors need to be explored. Choice or predisposition is not always clear in assessing sexual addiction. The question here is why an individual engages in sexual activities knowing that there are certain consequences, running the risk of

20. Carnes, *Don't Call It Love*, 23–24.
21. Silverman, *Love Sick*, 16.

6

self-destructive behavior. Case studies show that individuals involved in high-risk sexual activity feel invisible or invulnerable, believing they are not at risk.[22] Yet, the risk may be part of the excitement, creating a further high, a rush of adrenalin as part of sex. A means sought to solve the problem of unrestrained sexual activity, apart from marriage is religion. However, the way marriage is seen as a solution that can exacerbate the problem is also true for religion, when the underlying factors causing the addiction have not been examined such as guilt and shame.[23]

The ongoing desire to put an end to the sexual acts characterizes the fifth sign of sexual addiction, especially in what surfaces as "involuntary" sexual acts.[24] The conscience reminds the individual that this will be the "last time"—an admission that the act must stop, and at the same time, permission to perform the act once again. Putting an end to sexual activity may be an attempt to reduce the frequency of sexual acts, or, discontinue the acts completely; yet, in both instances, the addict is met with failure, managing sobriety for a day or two, and then acting out worse than the previous state, where the individual falls into compulsive sexual behavior.[25]

"Sexual fantasy" as the sixth category represents a coping mechanism to deal with the obsessive sexual desires. While fantasy may appear to be a way of dealing with desires, the imaging process exacerbates the need for sex creating a vicious cycle between fantasy and acting out. The problem with sexual fantasizing is that the addict may use this escape to avoid acting out, so it may seem that the addict is taking control of the condition. Sexual fantasizing is difficult to evaluate since fantasies cannot easily be measured to determine whether they constitute a serious problem, or some kind of disturbance in the day to day activities, or simply an

22. Carnes, *Don't Call it Love*, 17–18.

23. Shame will be treated in the following chapter. See also Bradshaw, *Healing the Shame*, 154–59.

24. Carnes, *Don't Call it Love*, 19.

25. In one instance, an individual I was counseling maintained he succeeded abstinence for about one week, then, collapsed into obsessive sexual fantasizing, pornography and finally, compulsive masturbation over the course of a day, compensating for the sobriety of the previous seven days.

interruption to recover from boredom. Nevertheless, while sexual thoughts, fantasies and images may be a way of dealing with stress and pressure, these mental processes are not the same as sexual acts. With the buildup of sexual imaging and fantasizing, sexual release is ultimately sought, and this release is referred to clinicians as "acting out" which can range from compulsive masturbation, to casual sex, or starting a new sexual affair.[26] Although sex does not involve any drugs, it does have drug-like effects, comparable to the effects of morphine or heroin where the pleasure centers of the brain are stimulated.[27]

Precocious sexual patterns of children, often due to an abusive environment, sets the addict off to an early start in sexual binging, compulsive masturbation, increasing pornography, seeking prostitutes, one-night-stands, from heterosexual to homosexual encounters, it would appear that "increase" in sexual experience is needed to keep the addict going.[28] This seventh sign is one where the intensity of the sexual fix increases over time, especially when these sexual experiences have punctured the individual's childhood.[29] Narcissistic tendencies are often assessments given by psychologists and psychoanalysts to account for addiction.[30] Seeking a solution, addicts will turn to marriage when in fact, the monogamous relationship exacerbates the problem. The monogamous and restrictive character of marriage leads the addict to fantasizing and acting out within or outside of the marriage, and as a result compulsive masturbation within marriage is common among addicts.

---

26. Carnes, *Don't Call it Love*, 22.

27. See also Milkman and Sunderwirth, *Craving for Ecstasy*, 45. In humans, "any imbalance that would lead to a deficit in dopamine would produce anxiety and a craving for substances (alcohol, cocaine, heroine, amphetamine, etc.) or activities (gambling, crime, promiscuous sex, hang-gliding) that would temporarily restore this deficit" (36). Milkman and Sunderwirth maintain that "addictive drugs and compulsive problem behaviours share the common effect of increasing levels of dopamine" (39).

28. Carnes, *Don't Call it Love*, 23–24.

29. Carnes, *Don't Call it Love*, 23–24.

30. Milkman and Sunderwirth, *Craving for Ecstasy*, 24; Engler, *Personality Theories*, 181.

"Change of mood" is associated with the eighth sign of addiction. However, change of mood can have different causes and not just sexual ones. If a person associates sex with shame and guilt, certainly the mood will not be good, and shame only serves to reinforce the addict, since the more shame, the more guilt. Mood is, nevertheless, another highly subjective category. What leads to the mood change can be several factors, especially those underlying the addiction. If, for example, sex has been associated with shame, then, the individual cannot experience a sexual act without finding something wrong or without feelings of guilt.[31] This may have less to do with addiction, and more to do with how the individual was socialized. The mood change reflects a person who is hurting, but this pain can be the result of blurring love and sex, the pain that is the result of sexual abuse as a child, the unresolved psychological difficulties encountered as a child where parental love had been absent and finding some kind of substitute through compulsive sexual behavior. The mood changes are indicative of fundamental underlying problems that need to be considered.

Shame has a significant role to play in sexual addiction. Shame is that which "drives" the sex addict's behavior.[32] The addict is pulled between what is "right" and what is "sought." This leads to the experience of pain since what is right impedes the addict to seek sexual gratification, but once gratification is sought and obtained, then, there is the guilt. And so, the sex addict moves from pain to guilt.

The ninth category identified with sexual addiction concerns time. The significant aspect of sexual obsession is the time that goes into fantasizing and sexual imaging, sexual preoccupation, that is, just "being" or "feeling" sexual. Sexual obsession is also the preoccupation with time-consuming sexual detail suggestive of obsessive-compulsive sexual patterns, as in a case study of a sociology professor,

---

31. As argued in Bradshaw, *Healing the Shame.* Sex can also have a mood-altering effect as a drug, as explained above in Milkman and Sunderwirth.

32. Bradshaw, *Healing the Shame,* 34–38. Bradshaw argues how shame is the cause of narcissistic disorders. See also Appendix A in Bradshaw.

Mr. A stated that finding just the right kind of picture might sometimes take hours. The man in the photo needed to be dominant . . . once he found a picture that was "just right" he would masturbate to orgasm. He had long been aroused by this kind of picture and had a collection of similar photographs but was continually looking for new material.[33]

Related to time-consumption is the recovery from sexually acting out, whether this is due to guilt and shame, or anticipating the next sexual encounter. Prostitution, anonymous sex, cruising in parks, bookstores, bathhouses and gyms, webcam sexual addiction, time is a significant factor in terms of loss in all the fantasizing, planning and acting out. But, the amount of time spent on sexual matters suggests something subjective: what constitutes a lot of time will be determined by sexual needs which differ from person to person. Yet, a kind of non-functionality is suggested with energy that goes into the sexual experience from fantasies to acting out, neglecting family relations and work commitments.[34] While time can be objectively measured, whether this constitutes a real loss is subjective depending on the priorities of the individual, what constitutes too much time for one activity as opposed to others, and whether time used for sexual activities is a real loss if this corresponds to the needs of an individual.

Finally, as a tenth and final sign, the sexual behavior of addicts leads to the neglect of social and occupational responsibilities. If time, thoughts and energy are entirely sexually-oriented, the inevitable disequilibrium of a person's activities has the consequences of failing to assume daily responsibilities. Moreover, given the moral implications of sexual addiction, an addict would be confronted with ongoing situations in which lying is the only way out. The failure to assume responsibilities, and the connected lying as a way of accounting for such failures, can only reinforce a cycle

33. Stein et al., "Hypersexual Disorder," 1591.

34. As in the case study where Mr. A.'s compulsive masturbation meant he failed to reach orgasm if he had sex with his wife the same evening. Stein et al., "Hypersexual Disorder," 1590.

of pain, acting, out, guilt, shame, cover up . . . Yet, before one is to assume that the neglect of family or professional responsibilities is the result of sexual addiction, one would need to consider whether an unfulfilled marriage or dissatisfying career is not exacerbating an underlying psychosexual condition. Sexual addiction may be the effect of lack of fulfillment rather than a cause.

Research indicates that the family environment, early childhood experiences, especially in terms of how sexuality was first experienced/understood, a genetic disposition to addiction, an abusive environment, or childhood exposure to pornography, predisposes the individual to causal factors of addiction.[35] Cucci emphasizes the role of the family in relation to "self-image," "relations," "needs" and "sexuality."[36] In the case of therapeutic treatment of an eleven year-old pre-adolescent with heavy pornographic viewing was effected with symptoms of Post-Traumatic-Stress Syndrome—severe consequences of sexual addiction.[37] Adolescents overpowered by negative feelings find a desperate means to free themselves from overwhelming negativity which is manifested in "promiscuous and random sex, sexual offending , compulsive use of pornography or compulsive masturbation."[38] My aim is to consider these ten signs and offer a moral evaluation by re-interpreting the signs, followed by paths of support for the addict.

## Re-interpreting the Signs

My interest in this section is to re-interpret these signs in the light of the identified patterns.[39] These signs can be re-grouped into

35. The impact and implications of casual sex on children is studied in McIlhaney and McKissic Bush, *Hooked*, 49–72.

36. Cucci, *Dipendenza Sessuale Online,* 41, builds on Guerreschi's findings, *Dipendenza Sessuale,* 79.

37. Pellai, "La cittadinanza intima," 25.

38. Longo et al., "Effects of Internet Sexuality," 94.

39. The American Society of Addiction Medicine gives five characterizations of addiction. It should also be noted that in their public policy statement of April 12, 2011, the ASAM regarded addiction as a "primary, chronic disease

three main categories: (i) "repeated" sexual acts, (ii) "out-of-control" behavior, and (iii) "severe consequences." These three signs express the fragility of the human condition—the brokenness that is in need of God to find hope and ultimately freedom.

## Repetition of Sexual Acts

As I maintained above, what constitutes "repeated" acts as a sign of addiction cannot be taken in isolation from the two other signs following, "out of control" and "severe consequences." In other words, repeated acts alone are insufficient to identify an addiction, however, the repetition of unwanted acts, that suggests a sexual pattern of involuntary behavior, moves into the direction of sexually compulsive behavior. Frequency suggests hypersexual activity, but such activity that is volitional and perceived as inconsequential cannot, therefore, constitute addiction.[40] Out-of-control behavior, that is, its non-volitional character, suggests the emergence of an addiction.

## Out-of-Control Behavior

Patterns of out-of-control behavior have been a central element in identifying addiction. Out-of-control behavior is experienced by the suffering individual; the person cannot live how they want to live because of their psychological fragmentation expressed in their sexually addictive acts. "Out-of-control" behavior as a sign remains a constant indicator. Yet, in an attempt to fulfill sexual needs the person is expressing an emotional need, as I have shown, in reference to Sue Silverman's experience. The sexual addict is

---

of brain reward, motivation, memory and related circuitry" ("Definition of Addiction," 1). Neurobiological considerations will be taken up in the next chapter.

40. The American Psychiatric Association, in identifying Psychosexual Disorders, considered "repetition" with other psychological factors as part of the characteristics, (DSM-III, 1980; DSM-III-R, 1987; DSM-IV, 1991; DSM-IV-TR, 2000; DSM-V, 2010). See, Kafka, "Hypersexual Disorder," 378.

seeking for the love that is not there, or that has not been known, and they are still seeking. It is this fundamental premise that leads to offering help to the sexual addict: an emotional need sexually expressed. This need is as much emotional as it is spiritual given the brokenness of the human condition.[41] Related to this second sign, is the fifth sign, the ongoing desire to limit or bring under control sexual activity.[42] The sixth sign, obsessive sexual fantasizing and imaging as an escape mechanism is also out-of-control behavior given its obsessive nature. Since the fantasizing resembles addiction to pornography where fantasies are produced by external images, the end result in both cases is a sexual outlet, either masturbation or seeking sexual partners. The seventh sign, increasing sexual experiences to heighten sexual gratification further suggests out-of-control behavior.

## Severe Consequences

The second, third, fourth and eighth signs all refer to consequences that are involved. While the third conveys consequences connected to out-of-control behavior, the fourth is more high-risk behavior.[43] The severe consequences to the sexual behavior suggest

41. I will return to this issue in the last chapter of my work.

42. I am treating the first, fifth, sixth and seventh signs as one category of signs since they all concern more or less "control."

43. Signs two, three, four, eight, nine and ten, I am regarding as one category of signs since they all refer morally to consequences. In the case of the fourth sign where high-risk behavior is involved, this involves having sex with sexual partners with AIDS and STDs. The psychological aspect to this fourth sign is that the individual somehow feels invulnerable—nothing will happen to them. See Carnes, *Don't Call It Love*, 18. The eighth sign which involves "mood change" is also a consequence of sexual addiction. Mood-change operates in both directions, as a trigger for sex due to depression, or as a result of the acting out, as in shame. A difference is pre-supposed in the "mood change" caused by "acting out," and a mood change/disorder that triggers the "acting out." See the American Society of Addiction Medicine, "Definition of Addiction," 4. The need for sex as "medication" already expresses a disordered mood condition. The ninth and tenth signs, similarly, time spent, and neglect of responsibilities, are both consequence of sexual activities.

that if there are no consequences, there is no sexual addiction. A wealthy person who has an "open" spouse/relationship may not have to worry about a spouse or employment as consequences. Yet, the individual may be obsessed with sex (due to boredom), watching pornography, then, compulsively masturbating, engaged in cybersex, leading possibly to multiple sexual partners, without any apparent consequences. In this respect, the consequential behavior is less reliable than out of control (where the behavior is "unwilled"). Why the excessive need for sex outside of marriage, and in forms that are non-conjugal (pornography, masturbation, cybersex)? The question arises whether the individual is seeking the fulfillment of emotional needs, rather than sexual ones. This is also true for the ninth and tenth signs where "time" factor is an issue in obtaining sexual material; the compulsive sexual behavior leads to time loss, and neglect of one's responsibilities, respectively, which can be adequately subsumed under "consequences."

Three inseparable signs, therefore, can be identified with sexual addiction, repetition of sexual acts, out-of-control behavior, followed by severe consequences. The causal aspect of addiction is not treated as a sign, since it is the surface behavior that is present. We have seen that environmental causal patterns that predispose a person to addiction range from the family's attitude towards sexuality to sexual abuse. In the following chapter I will consider further psychological factors as well as neurobiological ones as potential underlying causes.

If we consider severe consequences, ranging from sexually transmitted diseases to job loss and marital failure, as the result of involuntary repeated sexual acts, we are left to explore an underlying cause or causes of sexual addiction. Psychosexual and neurobiological factors cannot be overlooked in the emotional and sexual development of the individual, starting from childhood, as well, as how pleasure is triggered and experienced in the human body with all its implications.

# 2

# Underlying Factors
# and Manifestations
# of Sexual Addiction

In chapter 1 I examined the signs of sexual addiction as well
the possible causes. Factors associated with childhood family
history are in themselves viewed as a sign that may predispose
the individual to compulsive sexual behavior. I also re-examined
and re-grouped ten signs of addiction, reducing them to three inseparable indicators of sexual addiction, namely, repetitive sexual
acts, out-of control behavior, and severe consequences. In chapter 2, I examine sexual addiction in the light of psychoanalysis,
and neurobiological studies, the underlying factors and related
manifestations.

## Neurotic Tendencies

From a Freudian perspective, pleasure initiates with excitement
that is interpreted by the subject as a desire that needs to be satisfied removing the tension that excitement causes. With each satisfaction there is a specific corresponding act which is significant in
its quality in terms of the nature of the act—"what is remembered

is the pleasure."[1] It was Ferdinand de Saussure who made the distinction between two experiences of pleasure, the affect of pleasure and the sentiment of pleasure.[2] The difference between affect and sentiment is significant: the former includes impulses of culpability or shame, and aggressiveness towards the self, while sentiment belongs to the secondary system as in temptation not because the person has a need for the desired object, such as food or drink, but simply the attraction to the object. The distinction shows that a person has real basic needs to be fulfilled, and to obtain the satisfaction of these needs. The need to drink and eat are linked to self-preservation and survival. However, there are also needs to be fulfilled at a more "psychological" level, the result of anticipated pleasure, and equally creates a need for satisfaction.

A person's sexual desire may be the result of a sexual attraction, and leads the person to engage in sexual activity, but it is the person that is desired, rather than the need for the sexual act, that is at the level of the Saussurean notion of sentiment. This is clear with food, when a person eats not out of hunger, but because the object is desirable, such as a fruit or a chocolate.[3] While the "I" evolves from an "I" principle of pleasure to an "I" principle of reality, whereby the sexual instincts recognize a change from initial auto-eroticism to a multiplicity of intermediate phases, to a love of the object and a service to procreation, failure to distinguish these fundamental sexual drives and needs means the individual remains at a narcissistic level of sexual pleasure.[4]

The seemingly irresistible movement towards sexual pleasure due to both biological and psychic factors is reinforced with sexual experience thus seeking repetition. The delay in this evolution from the "I"-principle to the "reality"-principle, either due to auto-eroticism or a latency period for an extended time, the principle of pleasure from which many individuals cannot detach themselves

1. Treatment on pleasure as interpreted by De Saussure, "Metapsychologie du Plaisir," 649.
2. De Saussure, "Metapsychologie du Plaisir," 647.
3. De Saussure, "Metapsychologie du Plaisir," 657.
4. Freud, "Formulations," 14–15.

disposes the person to neurosis.[5] The principle of pleasure can also experience failure when the need for pleasure is overlooked which occurs in neurosis. It is when pleasure is identified with an intense struggle and is repressed that neurotic forms of behavior manifest themselves as in masochism; either that which causes pleasure provokes displeasure, or that which causes displeasure provokes pleasure. The neurotic experience of pleasure needs to be treated so that the individual who experiences displeasure is freed from that which may be repressed.

Such neurotic symptoms may also account for sexual addiction, as shown in chapter 1, the indicators may vary, as well as factors causing or contributing to the sexually compulsive behavior, although I have reduced the signs to three. Sexual repression would be an overarching factor manifesting itself in the different signs of addiction. Sexual repression suggests unhealthy and alienating sexual practices may be a cause in addiction, and what shows up are the signs expressed of the repressed past of the individual, whether this is due to shame or sexual abuse.[6]

Morality bound to duty is found in Freud's psychoanalysis which also de-emphasizes the pursuit of the good—an attraction to the good because it is good. The Freudian *superego* resembles the individual governed by rules; a person is good because they act dutifully, even in suffering—the more it costs, the greater the moral act is.[7] In psychoanalytic terminology this is a kind of sado-masochism of the *super-ego;* these cases of neuroses may be the result of environmental conditions and an attitude towards sexuality associated with shame.[8]

---

5. Freud, "Formulations," 17–18.

6. I am suggesting that both shame and sexual abuse function as dispositions towards sexual addiction. Shame is covered in the next section.

7. The role of duty and obligation will be taken up in greater detail in the next chapter.

8. Shame is further discussed below.

## Psychoanalytical Framework

Approaching sexual addiction from the perspective of psychoanalysis offers insight into what may be happening to the person at a deeper level, a level that is not accessible directly to the conscious. This unconscious level is the result of the early years of a child's psychosexual development and relationship with the parents (as I show below). These initial stages of psychosexual development do not disappear, but in fact, sexually structure the person which is why a psychoanalytical framework is extremely useful in examining sexual addiction.

Freud moved from the more traditional view of sexuality, putting aside Aquinas's conception that human sexuality served the primary purpose of reproduction, and all other purposes were relative to reproduction, and advanced the view that sexuality is fundamentally associated with pleasure.[9] Freud however, enlarged the notion of sexuality beyond that of genital activity to include whatever brought pleasure to the child such as thumb-sucking in a form of sublimation.

The Oedipus complex which is one of Freud's greatest findings basically states that a child unconsciously desires to possess the opposite-sexed parent and discard the parent of the same sex. The anxiety experienced by the boy towards the father who is a rival, and the mother whom he desires, leads to "castration anxiety." The resolution to castration anxiety is by identifying with the father, and therefore, the boy vicariously possesses the mother. The girl, instead, turns to the father, with "penis envy," whereby the mother is perceived as responsible for her effected castration. The girl ultimately, but reluctantly, identifies with the mother making the difficult transition from what is idealized to the reality of her castrated state.[10]

9. See Porter, *Natural and Divine Law*, especially, chapter 4, "Marriage and Sexual Ethics," which presents the evolving, conflicting views concerning sexuality and reproduction. The relationship between human sexuality and reproduction is discussed at length.

10. The story for the female counterpart has been significantly criticized by Bernsetin, "The Female Oedipal Complex," 183–217. Also, Small, "The

The lingering effects of any of the four stages, oral (birth to first year), anal (second year), latency (seven years to puberty), genital (puberty to adulthood) where the libido, the emotional and psychic energy resulting from the biological drive, is prevented from obtaining complete satisfaction in one or more of these stages, leads to a fixation or arrestation at one of these stages. Sexual disorders are the result of a fixated development besides an unresolved Oedipal conflict.[11] The *id* is the pleasure principle seeking tension reduction; the *ego* emerges to meet the demands of the *id*, but within the norms regulated by the outside world, thereby, functioning as a reality principle. The *superego* represents the internalized values, moral norms and standards developing through interaction with one's parents during the childhood period. The *superego* consists of two subsystems: the conscience (self-evaluation) and the ego-ideal (ideal self-image). It is the *ego* that attempts to regulate the two polar ends, the *id* and the *superego*, both going in different directions, the *id* demanding instant satisfaction, and the *superego* demanding rigid prescriptions. With these three psychic divisions each having contact with the conscious and the unconscious, most psychic activity occurs at the unconscious level. The result is that conflict is one of the key characteristics of the Freudian understanding of the self, which is not a very optimistic one, either, a personality that is self-divided.[12] In Freud's own iceberg metaphor, nine tenths of the psyche is "submerged" at the unconscious level.

Unconscious psychosexual factors may be a contributing factor in sexual addiction. I have shown the reinterpretations of signs need to take into consideration the different categories involved in sexual addiction, causal, moral and psychological. I will return

Psychology of Women," 872–78. For criticisms of the unresolved male Oedipal conflict see Bernstein, "Beyond Counter-Transference," 249–56. For criticism on Freud's research on scientific grounds (concepts open to falsification) see Grünbaum's work, *Validation in the Clinical Theory*.

11. Criticism of Freud's theory would be failing to consider social and cultural influences resulting in a kind of biological determinism. Richards, "The Future of Psychoanalysis," 347–69.

12. Engler, *Personality Theories*, 50.

to the psychological dimension of sexual pleasure in chapter 4. The biological and neurological aspects of sexual addiction will be further explored below to shed light on the moral implications of sexually compulsive acts.

## Neurobiological Studies of Sexual Pleasure

At the neurological level dopamine is the key ingredient of what the individual is experiencing. The Ventral Tegmental Area (VTA) of the midbrain is where the neurotransmitter dopamine is manufactured and sent to the higher brain regions acting as a neurochemical transmitter signaling to focus and responding to the sex drive, and with the release of dopamine, pleasure is experienced.[13] Testosterone is the hormone that prepares the body and brain for sexual activity.[14] The cortex is found in the forebrain where complex thoughts arise including abstract thought, language and consciousness.[15] The dopamine release which occurs during orgasm results in euphoria which is in the VTA and the cortex, the same areas where pleasure is experienced during eating, drinking, cocaine, marijuana.[16] The power of the mood-altering experience due to the orgasm is sufficient to trigger an addictive pattern in the individual if other criteria are present such as lack of intimacy, loneliness, unresolved Oedipal conflicts, and so on. In fact, such conditions are common among people, and along with the libidinal nature of the person seeking pleasure and gratification, a predisposition to sexual addiction is already present.

13. Melis and Agriolas, "Dopamine and Sexual Behaviour," 19–38; Berridge and Winkielman, "What Is an Unconscious Emotion?," 181–211.

14. Testosterone is the hormone driving sexual desire. Since there are significant variations of testosterone among males, it can also explain why "sex drives" among men vary. This is an important consideration in understanding why some men appear more virtuous than others when it comes to exercising sexual abstinence: some men simply have less testosterone to deal with.

15. Struthers, *Wired*, 29.

16. Struthers, *Wired*, 95–97.

A Public Policy Statement defining addiction by the American Society of Addiction Medicine (ASAM) maintained that "addiction is a primary, chronic disease of brain reward, motivation, memory and related circuitry."[17] Taking into account the neurobiology of addiction, the ASAM recognized that "addiction is more than a behavioral disorder," and even questioned whether sexual addiction is a behavioral disorder by considering five characteristics of addiction (ABCDE): (i) Abstinence incapacity; (ii) Behavioral impairment of control; (iii) Craving increase; (iv) Diminished recognition of severe problems; (v) Emotional response dysfunction.[18] From what has been said these neurobiological factors may also account for the underlying neurosis of the individual in sexual compulsion, besides the environmental factors that may also serve to trigger the addiction.

## Dealing with Shame[19]

Associated with sexuality is often a personal and general culpability and shame. This kind of emotional culpability needs to be distinguished from true moral culpability which in a pastoral scheme leads to contrition. Emotional culpability does more harm than good when it becomes obsessive as one finds with masturbators.[20] This culpability has two effects, first to hide oneself from the moral authority, and second, shame creates a sense of indecency. Sexuality is often experienced with anger and cruelty at a more pathological level.[21] Erikson maintains that shame as an emotion has been inadequately studied because in western culture shame has been "absorbed by guilt."[22] Shame is associated with exposure,

---

17. American Society of Addiction Medicine, "Definition of Addiction," 2.

18. American Society of Addiction Medicine, "Definition of Addiction," 2.

19. In French *pudeur* and Latin *pudicitia* have the sense of virtue. *Verecundia* has the meaning of "bashfulness" compared to the French sense of *honte*.

20. Plé, *Vie Affective*, 181.

21. Plé, *Vie Affective*, 19.

22. Erikson, *Childhood and Society*, 227.

and thereby, feeling "self-conscious" and this shaming exacerbates the sense of feeling "small."[23] Researchers have considered the role of shame in contributing to addiction, and sexual addiction being one of them.[24] Shame is not always bad, nor is it always good. In this respect, shame can be divided into two types, good/positive shame and a bad/negative shame. Good shame is when a child grows up experiencing shame for what is wrong because the parents show disapproval of the child's actions, for example, a child is admonished by the parent for refusing to return a toy that belongs to someone else. The child feels shame for having taken something that does not belong to him/her. Bad/negative shame is when a child is made to feel shame for his or her feelings, these feelings are rejected, for instance, a child who spends a Saturday morning with a friend and is made to feel guilty wasting time, and feels shame for having misused his/her time. Rather than affirmation there is negativity and shame. The bad shame sets in when the child is made to feel shame for the feelings that are experienced, emotional or sexual, and treated as wrong. Bad/negative shame sets in especially in initial friendships that are looked upon with suspicion, such as a boy who is scolded for playing with a female friend. When an adult feels shame for being attracted to a married person this is good/positive shame because the individual is already in a committed relationship. But if the same adult feels shame after having sex with his/her own spouse, this is negative/bad shame because it is natural to have sexual intercourse with one's own spouse, provided this is by mutual consent.

Shame begins in early childhood experiences. Some children are valued not in terms of who they are but what they do. Added to "doing" things, what is done must be done well; the child is brought up in an environment of *facere* instead of *essere* and love is confused with doing things well. As an adult, this kind of negative/bad shame is where the individual feels inadequate regardless of how high the accomplishment/performance. The lack

23. Erikson, *Childhood and Society*, 227.
24. Carnes, *Don't Call it Love*, 94–101.

of affirmation, the ongoing feeling of insecurity due to negative shame needs some kind of outlet. Sexual habits become a satisfying psychological outlet that has the risk of turning into an addictive pattern.[25] A shame-bound person is one whose feelings, needs, drives are interpreted as shameful; this results in a lack of acceptance of who the person is and what the person does.[26] Parents love their children not only through affirmation but also by setting boundaries, reinforced by consistency, and with reasonable consequences when boundaries are crossed. Instead, when children have to figure things out for themselves, and if parents are not emotionally present for their children, they create a fear of abandonment (also in cases where parents have left the home).

Sexual addiction is often identified with "abandonment issues" where as an adult the person feels unlovable (because they knew abandonment). The worse damage for children is when parents tend to be very critical and attack by name-calling, "lazy," "dummy," leading to self-critical labels.[27] The role of the parents is fundamental in the good/bad shame experience of a child growing into adolescence. A dysfunctional family environment itself may trigger sexual escape-mechanisms as a way of coping but also as a way of relating to oneself and others, and this is also true for families that are rigid and disengaged.[28]

## Ego-Defense Mechanisms

Within the Freudian framework of psychoanalysis, defense mechanisms are pertinent to our discussion. These psychological defenses serve as a coping mechanism for anxiety, using one or several mechanisms. Defense mechanisms may become maladaptive even

25. Carnes, *Don't Call it Love*, 94.

26. A study conducted by Dr. David Olson of the University of Minnesota's Family Social Science Department claims that 78 percent of sex addicts come from "rigid" families and doing things "right" in such families is a priority. In Carnes, *Don't Call it Love*, 97.

27. Carnes, *Don't Call it Love*, 99.

28. Carnes, *Don't Call it Love*, 137.

destructive when they are used at the exclusion of all others or to an extreme, preventing personal and social growth.[29] We shall see that with sexual addiction, one of the most recurring, if not dominant, ego-defense mechanisms is that of repression which blocks traumatic experiences from the past that would otherwise produce anxiety. Repression is also a means of attempting to cope with traumatic experiences, thereby preventing the emergence of past traumas into consciousness. The other ego-defense mechanism used is denial so that the individual does not admit how sexual dependency can actually harm them, seeking to justify their behavior as normal. Unlike alcohol and drug abuse, sexual addiction cannot be measured by its consequences pertaining to health. This makes denial an easy defense mechanism on the grounds that the sexual conduct, pornography, masturbation and multiple sexual partners respond to personal needs and drives, with the claim this is a matter of free choice.[30] Negative transference may also be expressed in unresolved Oedipal conflict manifesting itself in multiple sexual partners, the result of an emotionally traumatizing childhood due to either parent, so that sexual partners become the object of sexual negativity, and sexual gratification is an attempt to resolve these conflicts.

The Diagnostic and Statistical Manual of Mental Disorders (DSM) classified sexual addiction as a "Hypersexual Disorder" in DSM-V.[31] The proposed criteria for Hypersexual Disorder are the following: over a period of six months, sexual fantasies, sexual urges, and behaviors which are associated with at least three of the following conditions: time consumed with sexual activities interfering with daily obligations; repetition of sexual activity due to dysphoric moods (boredom, depression, anxiety); repetition of

29. Erdelyi, "Defense Processes," 761–63.

30. Multiple sexual partners as a sex addiction is distinguished from pornography and masturbation, although these forms of sex addictions are interconnected as are other forms of addictions. Multiple sexual partners is not the same thing as "casual sex." Multiple sexual partners suggest a repetitive/addictive pattern due to a "need" to be satisfied that differs from substance use but has the same effect in terms of pleasure. See the section following.

31. Kafka, "Hypersexual Disorder," 377–400.

sexual activities due stressful events; repetitive but unsuccessful efforts to control sexual behavior; repetition of sexual behavior failing to consider emotional and physical harm to oneself or another. In addition to the time factor of six months, associated with at least three of the categories proposed by Kafka, two other factors come into place, "personal distress or impairment" in social or occupational functioning (or other areas) due to obsessive-compulsive sexual behavior, and finally, the sexual behavior is not the result of "exogenous substance."[32]

## Behavioral Expression

The behavioral aspect of sexual addiction has been researched by numerical quantification of sexual outlets as an indicator of addiction.[33] The quantification of sexual frequency has been referred to as Total Sexual Outlet (TSO) by researchers. Studies have shown that few males, 5–10 percent of the samples studied have a TSO of five to seven times per week, and even this level of TSO cannot be sustained for long.[34] Based on such findings, Kafka maintains that sexual addiction would involve at least a TSO of seven times per week and sustained over a six month period. The disagreement between psychologists is whether a TSO seven times per week over a six month period is pathological and whether the term "addiction" can be applied.[35] The emotional and physical factors associated with sexual addiction, depression, instability in relationships as well as infections sexually transmitted in approximately 3–6 percent of the general population is cause for concern.[36] Sexual addiction manifests itself behaviorally in four particular areas, pornography, masturbation, cybersex and multiple sexual partners.[37]

32. Kafka, "Hypersexual Disorder," 379.

33. Dozois and Firestone, *Abnormal Psychology*, 324.

34. Kafka, "Hypersexual Desire Disorder in Males," 505–26. "TSO" refers to the total number of sexual outlets (orgasms).

35. Dozois and Firestone, *Abnormal Psychology*, 324.

36. Black, "Epidemiology and Phenomenology," 26–72.

37. Kafka also discusses "telephone sex" and "strip clubs." See Kafka,

## Pornographic Consumption

In the case of pornography a compulsive patterns sets in through sexual visual stimuli, followed by the sensory system of masturbating, and the neurological effects (orgasm). This pattern is stored and becomes a reinforced neurological habit.[38] The fantasizing associated with pornographic images increase testosterone production thereby, heightening sexual desire.

The definition of pornography taken from the *Catechism of the Catholic Church*, 2354, is as follows,

> Pornography consists in removing real or simulated sexual acts from the intimacy of the partners in order to display them deliberately to third parties. It offends against chastity because it perverts the conjugal act, the intimate giving of spouses to each other. It does grave injury to the dignity of its participants (acts, vendors, the public), since each one becomes an object of base pleasure and illicit profit for others. It immerses all who are involved in the illusion of a fantasy world.[39]

The Catholic Catechism gives a definition to pornography from different angles, descriptive, moral and psychological establishing why pornography cannot be acceptable in any form.

Rather than consider pornography as a potential target for individuals with existing sexual "hang-up," the insecurities that individuals have make pornography potentially threatening, as an escape leading to high-risk addictive behavior. It would be disastrous, and not only naïve, to think of pornography simply in terms of an outlet to experience pleasure, something that is part of the human being. Pornography has far reaching consequences not just because of the artificial means by which pleasure is experienced,

---

"Hypersexual Disorder," 387. There are also differences between male and female sexual addiction. For instance, "telephone sex" is more common among females. Kafka, "Hypersexual Disorder," 400.

38. Struthers, *Wired*, 99.

39. *Catholic Catechism* (#2354) in, Struthers, *Wired*, 29. This catechetical definition which Struthers considers reliable is the only definition that Struthers gives to pornography.

but also, the reconstruction of how reality is perceived, namely, individuals, and human relations.[40]

If the libido is the psychic pleasure principle which the *id* seeks to satisfy at all cost, one may ask where the moral problem lies in an individual engaged in sexual activity as "harmless" as pornography or masturbation, in the form of habits satisfying human sexual need. Nobody is excluded from libidinal impulses which are fundamentally part of the human being. Two factors are at work, however, one, the unconscious material whether this is an unresolved Oedipal conflict, a form of castration anxiety, or more traumatic experiences in terms of sexual abuse or a dysfunctional home, for instance, due to drug/alcohol dependency. The other factor plays or preys on the vulnerable psychic condition. Unlike having to go to a shop and purchase pornography where the risk of running into someone would be sufficient to deter the individual from venturing into a shop, the internet is immediate, private and even free.[41] A person may even be involuntarily exposed to pornography on the internet in the form of "pop-ups," and this may trigger subsequent visits to pornographic sites as a result.

Pornography, however, does not just disappear because it is deleted, and even if the viral pop-ups no longer appear, pornography is stored in the mind.[42] This is a crucial aspect of how pornography operates in individuals before an addiction takes place. Cybersex use may become ritualized or cyclical in nature.[43] When experience of viewing the pornography becomes part of a ritual—creating tension before and during the viewing, and the release of tension through masturbation and reaching an orgasm, the ritualistic pattern may lead to a dependent pattern if the earlier psychosexual factors discussed are present, such as repression, denial and/or a dysfunctional home setting.[44] Sexual nature

40. Struthers, *Wired*, 37–38.

41. The "Triple-A engine": accessibility, anonymity, affordability. Cooper, "Sexuality and the Internet," 187–93.

42. Struthers, *Wired*, 59.

43. Delmonico et al., "Treating Online," 154.

44. Struthers, *Wired*, 79.

which is far more than sexual organs and genital sex means the powerful libido encompasses a wide spectrum of human activity, but when this activity is oriented towards that which specifically brings sexual tension, this tension needs to be resolved. This is why pornography and masturbation are linked in sexual addiction. A person who is eventually dissatisfied with masturbatory practices will want to release this tension through cyber-sex and/or sexual partners.[45]

If human sexuality is expressed through intimacy in a way that conveys a bond between two persons, pornography which serves to arouse and excite by focusing on the sexual explicit material clearly distorts the value of human sexuality making it self-serving and exploitative. As a result, the feeling that is associated after viewing pornography and masturbation is one of shame.[46] These are two separate acts but which reinforce each other and leave the individual shame-ridden. These experiences are by no means those of self-worth and freedom, but growing self-deprecation and enslavement. The core of shame is that a person is not worthy of being loved.[47] If shame is a factor that leads to pornography, then pornography reinforces this negative self-image.

Since pornography sexually manipulates one's perception of reality, of oneself and others, by a heightened focus on the sexual, pornography creates an environment that pre-disposes the individual to sexual habits. This pre-disposition is largely due to the exaggerated perception of sexual activity in the general population in addition to a perception that premarital and extramarital sexual activity is frequent leaving the false impression that men and women are sexually promiscuous.[48] Sex addicts admit that they dislike the "out-of-control" feeling and time consumption associated with their pornographic activities.[49] Positron Emission

---

45. Cucci associates pornographic followed by cybersex addiction with an increasing escape from reality, *Dipendenza Sessuale Online*, 35–37.

46. Struthers, *Wired*, 55–56.

47. Struthers, *Wired*, 55.

48. Weaver, "The Effects of Pornography Addiction," 3.

49. Black et al., "Characteristics of 36 Subjects Reporting," 247.

Technology (PET-scan) of both pornography-addicted adults and non-addicted adults viewing pornography show brain reactions for both groups similar to cocaine addicts looking at image of people taking cocaine. These findings suggest that images that are emotionally arousing leave some imprint on the brain, which triggers instantly an involuntary, but lasting biochemical memory trail.[50]

The United States Attorney General's commission on pornography made the following observation,

> The myth about pornography is that it frees the libido and gives men an outlet for sexual expression which liberates mind and body. This is truly a myth. I have found that pornography not only does not liberate men but on the contrary is a source of bondage. Men masturbate to pornography only to become addicted to the fantasy. There is no liberation for men in pornography.[51]

Pornography offers not only for the curious mind to the sexually starving promises of sex, to intense orgasms and with the addictive patterns that ensue, it is the mood-altering experience that is ultimately experienced, sought and re-experienced in an endless pattern of endless sex. In fact, sexual addiction is really of a pathological nature because of the mood-altering experience and the sexual acting out further changes the emotional state of the person involved.[52]

## Masturbation

I have shown above the relationship between pornography and addiction, and how pornography can lead to compulsive masturbation. M. Kafka points out that in hypersexual addiction, masturbation is the most common "enacted lifetime sexual behavior."[53]

50. Rahey and Hagerman, *Spark*.

51. In MacKinnon and Dworkin, *In Harm's Way*, 180–81.

52. Ariely and Loewenstein, "The Heat of the Moment," 87.

53. Kafka, "Hypersexual Disorder," 381.

Masturbation can be the result of a habit, compulsive behavior where deeper problems of intimacy need to be addressed, preoccupation or impulsive urge.[54] Men who masturbate compulsively can be suffering from depression and a series of other mental problems.[55] In addiction the problem is not at the moral level concerning masturbation, but at a psychological level where masturbation expresses anywhere from repressed needs of intimacy to a denial that the person is an addict. The added risk arising from pornography is addictive masturbation is not only reinforced, but the further need of sexual pleasure—an endless cycle of need and gratification. In masturbation there is no "other"; the person is engaged in an ongoing sexual act with the self. The person is divided into parts, one which instrumentalizes the body to derive pleasure from it, and the other, where ecstasy is experienced. When the excitement leading to such pleasure feels exhausted, the risk the compulsive masturbator takes is triggered by internet pornography to reinforce the sexual excitement by further on-line sexual behavior.

## Cybersex Compulsivity

Besides online pornography there is the further difficulty of cybersex compulsivity which "involves more than simply engaging in online sexual activity."[56] Cybersex constructs a world disconnected from reality—a virtual world—in which sexual viewers/ participants are free to engage in erotic behaviors to satisfy their fantasies.[57] Cybersex makes use of webcams where people engage in sexual acts through cameras rather than through real physical contact; in chat rooms which becomes a major factor in time-consumption on the internet; or as shown above, the compulsive

54. Struthers, *Wired*, 169–70.

55. Carnes, "Cybersex, Courtship and Escalating Arousal," 45–78; Cooper et al., "Online Sexual Activity," 129–43.

56. Delmonico et al., "Treating Online," 148.

57. Delmonico et al., "Treating Online," 147.

viewing of pornography and acts of masturbation.[58] Cybersex is voyeurism at its best given the excitement aroused by viewing sex, and engaging in sexual acts with a video-cam/cybersex partner. If men are more vulnerable to using internet pornography than women, research shows that women are more inclined to use cybersex chat rooms than men.[59] This not only leads to cybersex addiction, but a greater risk in off-line sexual partners reinforcing addictive patterns.[60] With pornography/video-cam/cybersex addiction the increasing emotional distance further leads to estrangement between spouses.[61] Men and women view pornography differently. Men are more than six times as likely to view pornography as females and more likely to spend more time viewing it.[62] In cybersex studies women are more likely to have sexual encounters with their online companions compared to men. The reason may be explained that the male is more responsive to visual sexual triggers while the female is more inclined to be receptive to relational verbal queues.

In recent studies on men and women's sexual health, women use on-line chats for sexual purposes more than men which is supported by statistics showing that four out of five women and three out of five men believed that "texting, Facebook and other social networking tools" lead to promiscuous relationships, and men and women are more likely to engage in sex faster.[63] Studies show

---

58. Although differences between men and women and sexual behavior is beyond the scope of my study, research shows consistently that men and women function differently sexually, and this also includes pornography in the internet. See Young, *Caught in the Net*, 112.

59. Cybersex has the potential damage of real-life infidelity. See, Schneider, "Effects of Cybersex Problems on the Spouse and Family," 169–86, at 180.

60. Züllmann and Bryant, "Pornography's Impact on Sexual Satisfaction," 439–40, quoting Gutierres et al.

61. Studies have shown that about 30 percent lose their jobs, 40 percent of the sex addicts lose their spouses, and 58 percent experience financial loss, Layden, "Testimony for U.S Senate Committee," 2.

62. Stack et al., "Adult Social Bonds," 85.

63. Goldberg, "Social Working."

that 80 percent of women, and 58 percent of men, employ smart phones and laptops leading to faster sex.[64]

## Multiple Sexual Partners[65]

In this section I treat casual sex and multiple sexual partners differently; it is the latter sexual practice that I regard as addictive not because of the plurality of partners, since this may be true for casual sex, but rather, the signals that are present, stemming from early childhood that dispose the person to addictive patterns. The multiple sexual partners in sexual addiction represents a state of sexual activity where the person has lost control of their sexual behavior, and where risks are involved, and repetition is part of the sexual experience.

From the sections above, it should be clear that there is a relationship from pornography to multiple sexual partners, although, pornography leads to masturbation, masturbation does not necessarily lead to a plurality of sexual experiences. With cybersex, the risk that a person takes in addictive patterns increases. As sexually compulsive online users become bored, they take risks by seeking to meet partners offline.[66]

Multiple sexual partners stems from an early childhood environment where the person's sexual growth has been disturbed due to a number of possibilities, ranging from shame to sexual abuse. The solution to compulsive masturbation may seem to be marriage where the person is in a committed relationship, but if the elements of addiction are present, the person may be engaged in masturbation and sexual activity with their married partner, and then, look elsewhere once the sexual gratification is lost. This ongoing need for more sex, better sex, endless sex, drives the person. The person needs to explore what is being sought, and why sex is used as an escape. Silverman expresses this well in her book, that

64. Goldberg, "Social Working."

65. The clinical term is "Sexual Behavior with Consenting Adults." See Kafka, "Hypersexual Disorder," 379.

66. Delmonico et al., "Treating Online," 151.

she is looking for love, "Because I feel no real emotions, I manu-facture artificial ones. I seek comfort in this kind of sex I call love, which is all I know—all I've been taught—even as I don't *want* to know this."[67]

## Spiritual and Moral Perspective

In the preceding sections, I re-examined sexual addiction from the perspective of psychoanalysis, neurobiology and psychosocial studies. I have shown that sexual repression, denial and other ego-defense mechanisms linked to shame and a dysfunctional family setting may be factors triggering neurotic sexual patterns. The psychosexual condition of the individual, the result of early child-hood sexual experiences, and not just sexual abuse manifests itself in addiction, pornography, masturbation, cybersex and multiple sexual partners in an agonizing cycle:

---

. . . psychosexual needs>
        acting out>
                shame/guilt>
                        psychosexual needs> . . .

---

The resulting alienation and fragmentation of the person leads to recognizing a spiritual need—the need of being helped, making the right choices that will re-integrate the person with the self, with others and ultimately, with God: a personal human and spiritual re-integration. But help for a sexual addict presupposes that the individual recognizes there is hope, a way to recovery. Such hope rests in the belief that God's grace has the transforming power to help the person, as I show in the next chapter.

It is in the light of St. Thomas Aquinas that I will examine the moral implications of addictive sexual acts. The underlying psychological condition of the addict also needs to be considered

---

67. Silverman, *Love Sick*, 53.

in the light of this moral reflection.[68] The out-of-control behavior involves actions which the person does not intend. This "un-intentionality" is morally problematic; this will be examined within a Thomistic framework—to what extent actions can be said to be voluntary or involuntary? Aquinas offers a solution to these questions because he is concerned about human freedom, and how it is exercised. I will show that Aquinas provides elements of reflection as a possible "way out" of addiction in terms of habit, virtue, and overcoming vice. Through the moral re-structuring of the person the sexual addict may be led towards recovery. It is in the freedom of human acts that we can speak of moral theology. Finding a way out of addiction in counseling the addict requires an understanding of the challenges, but also the moral tension the addict experiences. In the next chapter I will look, therefore, at the moral structure of the person specifically in reference to Aquinas, thereby, offering a Christian response to sexual addiction.

---

68. The psychological factors cannot be overlooked, either, in what makes the addict act "involuntarily." I shall return to the psychological elements in subsequent sections of my work.

# 3

# St. Thomas's Moral Anthropology

In this chapter I shall explore different aspects of the person within a Thomistic framework. Nature, reason, appetite and the human end will be examined since the freedom of the human act is proper to moral theology.[1] Freewill plays a central role in the moral act. I shall examine the various questions that Aquinas poses concerning freewill, and the extent to which we may say the addict is free—or not free.

## Human Nature

Aquinas treats the nature of the person by considering the soul—the spiritual soul or the rational soul—specific to the human being.[2] The soul is a life principle, so, to be human is also to be a living creature. Fundamental to human nature are the powers of the soul; the intellective soul distinctly belongs to the rational creature. The intellective powers guide the sensitive and nutritive soul, while the nutritive soul depends on the sensitive and the intellective powers. In a hierarchical structure, below the rational

1. Aquinas, *Summa Theologiae* 1–2–7.2, *resp.* [Hereafter, *ST*, Part/s-Question-Article, *response/ad*—"reply to objections."]

2. *ST* 1–75.4, *resp.*

soul is that which employs the organs and drawing from extrinsic elements is the sensitive soul. Unlike the sensitive soul which has every sensitive body as its object, and also, unlike the rational soul which has the universal as its object, there is the vegetative soul whose operations are based on an intrinsic principle, limited to the soul to which the body is united.[3]

## Tripartite Soul and Reason

The tripartite soul represents the ways in which reason may or may not be present in the different faculties, intellective faculty, the sensitive, and finally, the vegetative, and whereby the faculties may be commanded. An act of command is an act of reason, which presupposes an act of the will, but reason precedes the act of the will, and conversely, the will also precedes reason. There is no precedence, neither in reason, nor in the will: reason reasons about willing just as the will wills to reason; however, command is an act of reason, while the first to move in the power of the soul performing the act is the will, while reason moves by the power of the will resulting that command is an act of reason moved by the power of the will.[4] In order for reason to carry out an act, to do something, there is a command, but this presupposes an act of the will, and so, preceded by an act of the will, reason moves to execute the act.

As shown above on "human nature" where the rational appetite reflects human specificity, the role of reason is fundamental in Aquinas's anthropology. Reason directs the individual to their end. Thus, leading the person to their end is the principle of human actions, and these actions belong to the deliberation coming from reason.[5] It is rational creatures that act for an end and since the will is to be found in reason, it can be said that reason

---

3. Aristotle, *De Anima*, 2.3–4 in *The Basic Works of Aristotle*. All Aristotle references are from *The Basic Works*.

4. *ST* 1–2–17.1, *resp.*

5. *ST* 1–2–1.1, *resp, ad* 3.

serves to act for an end.[6] Only creatures with reason can move themselves to an end because rational creatures can control their actions through their freewill.

## Appetite

The appetitive power is found in things that have knowledge; something may be apprehended as sensible or intelligible, while it is desired as something good. Each power of the soul has a natural inclination to something, while each power desires the object suitable for it.[7] Basing himself on Aristotle, Aquinas further maintains that the concupiscible and irascible obey higher parts, namely, reason and the will. The person is not immediately moved by the concupiscible or irascible appetites, but rather, waits for the will which is a superior appetite, in which the higher powers move the lowers ones.[8]

## *Exercise of the Will*

Aquinas makes the crucial observation that the will may act out of necessity and such an example comes from an end; for example, someone needing to cross the sea and wanting a ship for this purpose out of necessity. Similarly, the will inclining the person to the last end must out of necessity seek happiness.[9] Yet, the will does not desire whatever it desires out of necessity, this is because a person can be happy without certain things, and so, the will does not adhere to such things out of necessity. Drawing from Aristotle, Aquinas maintains that good and evil are in the object, and so, the will, attracted to a good or evil, is to be found in the object itself, while truth and error are objects of the mind. A thing that is good in itself is nobler than the soul in which the thing is un-

6. Aristotle, *De Anima,* 3.9.

7. *ST* 1–80.1, *resp.*

8. Aristotle, *De Anima,* 3.11.

9. *ST* 1–82.1, *resp.*

derstood, and in this respect, the will is higher than the intellect. The love of God is greater than the knowledge of God, while this is not the case for corporeal things where knowledge is better than the love of such things. Aquinas maintains that reason and freewill go together, otherwise, exhortations, council, commands, rewards, punishments . . . would be pointless. Because a person has apprehensive power, the individual can judge whether something should be avoided or sought.[10] A certain necessity exists in the will just as there is a necessity of the intellect: the latter adheres to first principles of truth, while the former adheres to happiness, the person's last end.

## Last End

Fundamental to the last end is the human being created in the image and likeness of God. Drawing from Augustine, Aquinas affirms that the person, created in God's image, must share in God's likeness, although, if there is likeness, it does not mean that the person is in God's image. In the person there is some likeness copied from God as exemplar—an image in reason although the likeness is imperfect likeness. Only intellectual creatures can share in God's image because of their intellectual soul, meaning that things without intellect are not made in God's image. This image includes God's divine nature as well as the Trinity of Persons to be found in the rational creature.[11] Aquinas further maintains that the rational creature is a likeness to God by way of an image in God's mind, while in other ways, a trace is present with the image of God being impressed in the human mind.

Actions performed by a person are actions that are truly human because the rational creature can master his/her own actions, and so, they are performed by persons who possess reason and freewill; these are human acts because the freewill engages reason. The assertion Aquinas makes regarding the end is that, "the object

10. *ST* 1–83.1, *resp.*

11. *ST* 1–93.5, *resp.*

of the will is the end and the good. Therefore, all human actions must be for an end."[12] For actions to be human, they must be voluntary. For this reason, "it is proper to the rational nature to tend to an end, as directing and leading itself to the end."[13] To show that there is not a plurality of ends, but only one end from which all other ends derive, Aquinas argues that there is a First Good as the end from which all ends flow.

## Faculties and Moral Acts

The faculties that involve human conduct cannot be separated from each other given the substantial union of the person, body and soul. The interconnectedness, or an interpenetration involves the tripartite soul from the inferior levels of the natural appetites to the superior levels of will and reason, and the intermediary level, moving between the superior and lower faculties, that of the passions, imagination and concupiscence. The moral act itself also needs to be considered and distinguished from the premoral act.

## Premoral Act

Aquinas develops the notion of imperfect human acts which can also be understood as a premoral act. The question concerning the perfection of the act, whether it is truly human, is connected to how free the act is, to what extent the free will is engaged. Premoral acts are determined by external factors where the will is not truly involved which is needed to choose the end, and judge the end, the knowledge and love of a particular object. The premoral or imperfect human acts also involve a focus on personal good rather than good for the other, including what brings personal pleasure and what does not. Even in friendship the motives may be for self-interest as opposed to a desire for reciprocity.

12. *ST* 1–2–1.1, *resp.*
13. *ST* 1–2–1.2, *resp.*

The objective nature of the human act refers to objective knowledge of the object and the means to attain the object. In the case of the imperfect human act the knowledge of the object is too subjective and too sensory to make an objective evaluation and judgment of the end, and of the means to obtain the end. Imperfect love is one that is moved more by fear than by true love. In situations where modesty, for example, is the result of societal expectation, and experienced with interior conflict, rather than a sense of a good that leads to God, modesty remains an imperfect moral act.

The natural appetite that is found in children that moves them towards the objects that bring them pleasure is natural, comes from God, and there is nothing wrong with this, given the stage of rational development in children. As they progress towards adulthood, children need to overcome narcissistic tendencies by posing human acts not just by seeking pleasure in itself. The appetite of the intelligence has as its object not in sensory pleasure, but the true good, not useful or pleasing, but a good sought in itself.[14]

As Albert Plé suggests, based on Aquinas's anthropology, four stages can be identified and differentiated in the moral development of the person: (i) at the infancy stage there is no moral act because there is no human act of a child at the premoral stage; (ii) the child is gradually capable of attaining the first human act discovering an ultimate and universal end to actions performed at which point the moral life begins; (iii) with increasing human acts, virtue is acquired as a *habitus* and a disposition orienting the individual to the ultimate end, but, there can still be division between reason and will due to the passions present at this stage, with most people remaining between perfect and imperfect moral acts; and finally, (iv) in this last stage the individual has reached a full development, exhibiting the capacity for stability and self-control, and the perfection of the moral act that leads the individual back to the Creator.[15]

14. Aristotle, *Nicomachean Ethics*, 10.3.

15. Plé, *Vie Affective*, 57–58.

Problems arise when animal passions are felt more intensely than spiritual joys.[16] Aquinas clearly makes the point of the integration of the person, the animal and the spiritual. The virtuous habits perfect the powers which allow for a better integration and harmonization of the person; virtuous acts serve to unify the different powers.[17] Virtues are connected in that they grow together, unlike the vices which are not connected, although the latter do generate each other in a disintegrated process, reinforcing a natural contradiction between spirit and body due to original sin, and which sanctifying grace purifies and elevates.

Sin is a moral disintegration or an absence of integration of the person, a conscious and free offence against the law of God.[18] Even if sin is at a purely material level, if the circumstances did not permit the will of the person to be engaged in a sinful act, the sin still causes the dissociation of the person. God's grace, precisely because it comes from God, enables the individual to act with interiority and self-determination that would otherwise not be possible for the sinner. From a theological perspective, maturity is perfection towards human and divine life. This movement is made possible through grace that transforms the person into a child of God, beginning at a biological level, then a psychological one, to human acts, and to virtuous ones, from baptism to this progressive power of integration to becoming a child of God.[19]

Freedom is found not in whether to obey or not to obey external laws, but from within, identifying that something is good with the aid of the intelligence, and pursuing this good. To pursue a sexual good, grace is needed so that the good to be enjoyed corresponds to the "natural law." The basis of the natural law is offered by Servais Pinckaers who states,

> Natural law had the obvious advantage of being accessible to reason and presenting a solidly and universally viable basis for the rational study of moral questions. It

16. *ST* 2-2-141.4.
17. *ST* 1-2-56.2, *resp.*
18. Sin will be dealt with in greater detail in chapters 3 and 4.
19. Plé, *Vie Affective*, 74.

also placed moral teaching within the tradition of the ancient Greek and Roman philosophy that had been adopted by scholasticism.[20]

If the intelligence recognizes the need to detach oneself from the good, then, grace is needed for this detachment. Grace is further needed to purify the mind and body in pursuit of what pleasurable good may be pursued, as well as those goods that produce sexual pleasure that need "letting go."

## Concupiscence

Given the nature of the appetitive powers of the soul, it may appear that involuntariness may be said to account for concupiscence. The human body and intrinsic principles proper to the body, may suggest involuntariness. For instance, thirst is part of the vegetative appetite and water is needed to sustain the body to survive. The desire to drink water corresponds to this natural need to survive. Concupiscence is at the level of the sensible appetite, but has the vegetative appetite as a source. So, the body's organs through which sensory experience is obtained responds to the desires of the natural appetite. The first involves only an intrinsic principle, while the second involves an extrinsic principle.

An Aristotelian interpretation of concupiscence from which Aquinas draws is that concupiscence diminishes the human capacity to reason; knowledge is fundamental to pose a moral act, especially in terms of judgment and prudence, then, it would appear that concupiscence "causes involuntariness."[21] Love belongs to the concupiscible power something specifically belonging to the appetite since the good is the object of both, the appetite and of love. The natural appetite arises from some object that is apprehended by the subject, seeking what is suitable according to the nature of the individual, by reason, and a nature put in them by God. The appetite arising from the apprehension of the subject

20. Pinckaers, *The Sources of Christian Ethics*, 291.
21. Aristotle, *Nicomachean Ethics*, 6.5.

is not from freewill but from necessity, as in animals, although in the case of humans, while there is a sensible appetite, the presence of reason can govern the appetite. The appetite following from an apprehension in the subject is called freewill. Love is found in each of the appetites—the movement towards that which is loved. In the case of the natural appetite, it would be the co-naturalness with the thing which is loved; sensitive love is to be found in the sensitive appetite, and intellectual love in the intellectual appetite. In each case the appetite pertains to the apparent good, and so, to the concupiscible power.[22] Concupiscible love and love of friendship need to be distinguished on the basis of things that are loved because they are desired—the good towards which one moves, loving something for oneself, and from loving someone to wish them good (including towards oneself).[23] Concupiscible love is not just loved for the thing itself but for something else, making it a relative good.

## Intellect and the Will

The intellect gives rational creatures their human specificity, and where the sensitive appetite is involved, the will is fundamental. It may seem that the will moves the intellect, as in a mover-moved relation, suggesting that the intellect is exercised when one wills it, thus, making it appear that it is not the intellect that moves the will.[24] Referring to Aristotle's *De Anima*, Aquinas reaffirms, "the appetible object is a mover not moved, whereas the will is a mover moved."[25] The desired object is a mover because it inclines the will, but the object itself is not moved, while the will that is moved, also moves the subject towards the desired object. Since it is the good which is the object of the will, the will moves all other powers of the soul to act. The intellect's role is fundamental because it is de-

22. *ST* 1–2–26.1, *resp.*

23. Aristotle, *Nicomachean Ethics*, 8.2.

24. *ST* 1–2–9.1, *ad* 3.

25. Aristotle, *De Anima*, 3.10.

termined or specified by the object that presents itself as a formal truth to the intellect: "truth is the object of the intellect," which in turn moves the will by presenting the object to it. Included in the universal truth is the good, as a particular good, and so, the intellect moves the will because some good is apprehended in the universal truth.[26]

A good moves the will while an object is apprehended as a good and suitable on the basis of two causes: (i) from the "condition" of the thing proposed, or to whom it is proposed; and (ii) how something appears to be suitable or unsuitable in different ways, "according as a man is, such does the end seem to him."[27] Aquinas concludes that the sensitive appetite can change according to the passions of the individual, that is, in a state passion, something may seem to be more fitting than when the person is not affected by a passion.[28] The sensitive appetite that is affected by an object moves the will. The will resides in reason, and it is reason that moves not only the will, but also the passions, the irascible and the concupiscible.[29] This would suggest that the will is not separable from a sexual act, nor is the intelligence.

In the case of sexual acts where the power of the will is diminished, since the will resides within the intelligence, the intelligence itself is not reduced. The problem is not one of whether the object is known for what it is, but whether the object is a good which it may not be. The role of reason in relation to concupiscence is fundamental to the human act. The fact that an object is desired means there is an inclination, and so, is moved towards the object to obtain this good. This inclination caused by concupiscence makes the act voluntary rather than involuntary. The power of concupiscence may seem to impair knowledge, that is, a person

---

26. *ST* 1–2–9.1, *ad* 3.

27. Aristotle, *Nicomachean Ethics*, 8.5.

28. Passion will be treated in detail in chapter 3 below.

29. The will does not act in a manner that is despotic like a master and slave, but more like a governor ruling over free citizens. This analogy shows that the irascible and concupiscible can act counter to the will, and so the will can be moved by them at times. See, *ST* 1–2–9.2, *ad* 3.

may not appear to be guided by reason, but this is only true in the cases where someone has been affected by concupiscence in such a way as having gone "mad," and then, one could speak of an act not being voluntary. Aquinas does not say that the converse is the case, either; it does not mean that a person who has gone mad due to concupiscence is acting involuntarily; this is because things lacking reason have neither voluntary nor involuntary capacities. The will exercised by the rational person can resist passion, and the will can choose not to act and not to will.

Aquinas reflects on moral activity by considering the "voluntary" and "involuntary."[30] Eight questions are asked that are also relevant for the purposes of this discussion: i) If there is anything voluntary in human acts?; ii) If there is anything voluntary in irrational animals?; iii) Can there be voluntariness without any action?; iv) Can violence be done to the will?; v) Can violence cause involuntariness?; vi) Does fear cause involuntariness? vii) Does concupiscence cause involuntariness? viii) Does ignorance cause involuntariness? The questions pertain to a person's freedom in moral activity. The degree of voluntariness serves to assess the disposition of the individual in the capacity to perform or refrain from an act. It is when acts become persistent or habitual in character, that is the focus of my discussion.

Human acts are end-oriented and movement towards an end requires knowledge of that end. The two principles operating, one extrinsic and the other intrinsic, show that a first principle is within the appetitive power of the individual, while it is moved by an extrinsic principle, that which triggers the act. The person acts voluntarily even when there is an external cause arousing the person and leading to bodily alterations, but this is not a direct cause on the person, but rather an indirect one, so the person still engages in a voluntary act. The question remains whether the will can be obstructed from being used, so that the moral act is not within the freewill of the individual. The possibility of something external that is more powerful than the will where some "violence"

30. *ST* 1-2-6.

is done to the will would impede the person from acting freely.[31] As I have indicated, the will can be regarded, using Aristotle's expression, as a "mover moved," in which there is both an active and passive force engaging the will, so it would appear that the will is also compelled to act.[32]

The will can also be understood as, (i) the "wish" of the will to elicit an act; and (ii) the act commanded by the will that is performed. Violence against the will—when the moral agent is refrained from acting freely—cannot be done to the will in the first sense, that is, when there is the wish to do something, but it can in the second where something prevents the will from performing an act. Violence is done to the will because of the powerful forces that appear to obstruct the will from performing what it sets out to perform. The distinction being made is between what moves the will that precedes from knowledge, and what moves natural appetite that does not precede from knowledge.[33] If the person acts on rational grounds, the will is said to be informed, while if the will acts out of appetitive impulses, the will is not informed, but the will is inclined towards an end, and in this case, that of pleasure.

## Passions

To understand the meaning that Aquinas gives to "passion" the term needs to be analyzed in relation to the attribute "passive": (i) whatever something receives (nothing is taken away); (ii) something is received (and taken away) making it better; and (iii) something is received (and taken away) making it worse, good health and poor health, respectively.[34] The nature of passion is to be found in the appetitive power drawn to things as they are in themselves, good or evil, while the apprehensive power is not drawn to a thing, but knows it intentionally, that is, as true or false, and exists in the

31. ST 1–2–6.4, *resp.*
32. Aristotle, *De Anima*, 3.10; ST 1–2–9.1, *ad* 3.
33. ST 1–2–6.4, *resp.*
34. ST 1–2–22.1, *resp.*

mind, not in the object.[35] Moreover, because passion is to be found where there is some corporeal transmutation, it is found in the sensitive appetite, and not the intellectual appetite.[36]

"Passions" treated by Aquinas as they are exercised in moral activity, that is, the place the passions have in the structure of the moral agent, are examined by considering four questions all related to the concupiscible. The concupiscible can be identified as "craving" for something in a meaning that is stronger than desire, for something that is pleasant. Craving presupposes that there is a pleasure to be experienced from the object that is craved. There is a twofold understanding of the human experience of pleasure: (i) the intelligible good that derives from reason; and (ii) the pleasure based on the perception coming from the senses. The distinction between the two is that in the first case the pleasure belongs to the soul only, while in the second, the pleasure belongs to both the soul and the body.[37] An object that produces sensible pleasure causes an attraction, which produces a love for the object.[38] The appetite, conforming to its nature, is shown in two ways: in the case where the object of love is absent, the appetite creates the concupiscence of the subject, and in the case where the object is present, the appetite creates pleasure in the subject.[39]

Two types of concupiscence in a subject can be identified, concupiscence of an irrational type, and concupiscence of a rational type. Irrational concupiscence reflects the animal appetite present in humans. In the first instance, concupiscence that is natural expresses the pleasure that is derived from something that is proper to humans and animals that which is "common and

---

35. Aristotle, *Metaphysics*, 6.4.

36. *ST* 1–2–22.3, *resp.*

37. Pleasure is covered in more detail below with reference to Albert Plé's work. Suffice it to say here that concupiscence is specifically this sort of pleasure—a craving for pleasure brought to the body and soul.

38. The tripartite distinction of the soul, as rational, sensitive and vegetative, has in each case the good as its end.

39. *ST* 1–2–30.2, *resp.*

necessary."[40] Rational concupiscence goes beyond the natural good for individuals, but that which is reasoned to be suitable. The rational concupiscence is "peculiar" and "acquired" because of the diversity found amongst individuals since different things are seen to be suitable.[41] The rational concupiscence, that is, the non-natural, can actually be infinite, compared to the irrational, or natural concupiscence which is finite. The irrational is finite because it corresponds to the needs of the body, and once those needs are met, one can no longer speak of an infinite concupiscence. In the case of the rational, however, because these desires proceed from reason, they can express the maximum possibility for the desires of wealth or sex.

In dealing with human sexuality, it is no longer either rational or irrational, but both, since both elements are present in sexual acts, that is, the dimension that corresponds to the sexual appetite which is natural in both humans and animals, and yet, the rational, in which one can reason the goodness of the sexual act and its repetition. Similarly, one can desire an accumulation of possessions, with little consideration for the means in which the wealth is obtained or disregarding the poor who are deprived of the basic needs for any well-being. This does not mean that natural concupiscence cannot be infinite, but it is one which is associated with a successive infinity, for example, after eating or having sex, still a desire more food and more sex. This natural and rational convergence is certainly true in the sexual domain where after engaging in sex and satisfaction is attained, there remains the desire for more sex—the desire for more, or simply repetition, which is a form of having "more of."

"Delight" is a passion, a movement of the sensitive appetite, and a perfection of the soul.[42] "Delight" is part of the appetitive power and enjoyment is the experience in taking delight in something. Beginning with the senses, these are the things that manifest

40. Aristotle, *Nicomachean Ethics*, 3.11; *ST* 1-2-30.3, *resp.*

41. Aristotle, *Nicomachean Ethics*, 3.11.

42. Aristotle, *Rhetoric*, 1.11. (The McKeon translation uses "pleasure" for "delight.")

themselves to us, offering some kind of appeal. The word that is used to understand "delight" is *fruitio* which has its origin in the word *fructus* "fruit" suggesting that to which the senses are attracted. There is also a kind of anticipation, an end that is in sight, the love or delight that one has in relation to this fruit or object. Aquinas maintains that since the end and the good are in the appetitive power, enjoyment must also be in the appetitive power.[43] A distinction is made between attaining the natural perfection, and the movement itself to this end. In the case of animals, their apprehensive capacities means they recognize their state of perfection, animal nature perceives when they become what is their nature, and this perception, is what is properly called delight. Pleasure means "becoming the nature of the thing."[44]

For Aquinas, only creatures endowed with knowledge can be goal-oriented and enjoy the end because the enjoyment is in the power that commands the achievement, and for this reason, things void of knowledge cannot "enjoy" their "end." Knowledge of an end is twofold, (i) perfect, in the case of rational creatures who know the good of the particular as well as the universal; and (ii) imperfect, in which only the end of the particular is known, this belongs to irrational creatures because their appetitive powers do not freely make choices, they do not freely command, but rather, move according to natural instincts to whatever they apprehend. Sexual acts are somewhere between the sensitive and natural appetite, they are naturally present within the person, not following any knowledge of an object, while the sensitive appetite responds to a good, based on the knowledge that it has of a good. The will is radically reduced responding to natural impulses in the presence of an apparent good.

An integration of the lower and superior appetites enables lower appetitive passions, with temperance and force, to become the principle human acts. In wanting the good, and the determination of the individual in pursuing this good, the person gives to the other appetites a superior end which transcends and ties

43. *ST* 1-2-11.1, *resp.*
44. *ST* 1-2-31.1, *resp.*

them together with harmony, so that, it is no longer the sensible appetite that desires, but the will that wants the desire, appropriates it, and the sensible appetite then becomes "human"; in this respect, the passions are integrated into the person and becomes part of the moral act. Such passions, then, emerge as the object of temperance and force. St. Thomas refers to human acts that extend to that which is "inferior" as *imperium* which employ both the intelligence and the will.[45] The sensitive appetite can be the principle of human acts when they are not guided by the will and reason. For a human act it is necessary and sufficient that the will is moved towards a good, but the passion that moves is the sign of a more intense will making the integration of passion into the human act more perfect.[46]

## Imagination[47]

A distinction can also be made between apprehension and the imagination; apprehension involves a specific object (particular) that is apprehended such as a tree, while imagination concerns a tree that is imagined (universal), suggesting that the imagination is closer to, or based on concepts. Both imagination and concepts rely on experiences of the particular. Apprehension may also occur, however without the command of reason since the sensitive appetite may be locked onto a particular object due to the imagination. For instance, due to the sensitive appetite, a person lusts, although the will does not seek to lust; there is an obstacle caused by the appetite where it struggles to submit to reason.

The body reflects a twofold relation in terms of the act of the sensitive appetite: bodily passions can be distinguished between the passions that precede, and physical response that follows. In this respect, the antecedent condition cannot be controlled, since it involves the nature of the sensitive appetite, but it is in the

---

45. *ST* 1–2–17.1, *resp.*

46. *ST* 1–2–74.4, *ad* 2.

47. The imagination in relation to lust will be taken up in chapter 4.

consequent that reason can be employed. Aquinas makes reference to St. Paul when referring to Romans, "But I am a creature of flesh and blood sold as a slave to sin. I do not understand my own behaviour; I do not act as I mean to, but I do things that I hate."[48] The natural and sensory appetites are distinguished but are interconnected. Reason commands through apprehension, and so acts that proceed from intellective or sensory appetites can be commanded, instead those having their source in the natural appetite cannot be commanded by reason such as thirst and sexual appetite. This would mean that since nutrition and generation belong to the vegetative soul, they are natural powers that cannot be commanded by reason. Both have an intrinsic character as indicated above; the difference is that in the case of sex, this appetite is triggered also by extrinsic factors that can be controlled.

## Internal Principles

The person who acts from within, that is, through reason and the will, without exterior influences or deliberately drawing from the exterior, is employing "internal principles." The interior disposition of a person which leads to making certain choices, can be examined in terms of disposition itself, as well as habit, distinguishing the single act from repeated acts. These internal factors of disposition and habit lead to both vice and virtue, as well as sin and holiness.[49]

## Habit and Disposition

"Habit" is understood as a "quality" in which a thing has as a disposition towards good or evil, either to itself or to something else.[50] This disposition as a habit is not the occasional act, but a regular

---

48. Rom 7:15, in *ST* 1-2-17.7, *ad* 1.

49. The dimension of holiness where a person overcomes their weaknesses and vices in pursuit of the good will be treated in chapter 5.

50. *ST* 1-2-49.1 *resp.*

recurring act which can be analyzed for its moral acceptability. A further distinction can be made between habits with natural dispositions, and others that are caused from the outside. The outside sort of habits are dispositions that cannot be easily lost or that are lost with difficulty due to their external cause.[51] The sub-division is also made at the level of the natural dispositions which can be either in potency or in act. In the case of natural dispositions as acts, may be "deeply rooted" or at the "surface level." It is in this category that sexual acts can be situated, as being natural, but either in potency or in act. As far as a natural disposition is concerned this is a disposition of what is natural to the person. Sexual impulses are natural in that they serve fundamentally to generate life. Yet, at a deep-rooted level sexual drives are identified with psychosexual factors.[52]

The disposition that the individual has may be towards good or evil which is reflected in how passions are expressed.[53] The basis of determining whether the passions are disposed to good or evil is whether this is suitable or unsuitable for the nature of the thing. The understanding of human nature is fundamental to give moral structure to the human agent. This makes the nature of the thing the basis of considering the dispositions. The nature of a thing is inseparable from the end and cause "why a thing is made."[54] Humans have a sexual nature, that is, sexuality is a fundamental constituent of humans, this is not only at an instinctive level that is found with animals, but one where reason is also present.[55] The disposition of a thing based on its nature has a finality. A habit, then, can be good or evil, easy or difficult. Finally, the distinction needs also to be made between habit (perfect) that has

51. *ST* 1-2-49.2 *resp.*

52. Psychosexual factors already presented in chapters 1 and 2 above; I will further take up deep-rooted sexual implication in subsequent chapters of my work.

53. *ST* 1-2-49.2, *resp.*

54. *ST* 1-2-49.2, *resp.*

55. To talk about a sexual nature is to talk about a sexual end. As shown above, all appetites have ends, and these appetites are intrinsic properties of the person expressed in powers of the soul.

lastingness to it, and disposition (imperfect) where such lasting-ness is not present.[56] In other words, a habit is perfect because it lasts, while a disposition is imperfect because it does not have such long-term duration.

Neither the body nor the soul is a disposition of habit, but rather the moral subject, the composite of body and soul.[57] Claims that "it is the power of my body" or the "desires of my flesh" that determine human acts would, from Aquinas's moral perspective, be erroneous assertions. The subject with this disposition to act is in a potential state, which is by definition what disposition is, some tendency towards an act, but until the act occurs, the subject re-mains in potentiality. The operation is performed through the soul followed by the body's physical motion. If this is a natural move-ment of the body, this is not a habit, because the "natural forces are determined by one mode of operation." It is by acts that habits are formed in which habits are in proportion to their operations.[58]

## Nature of Habit

The distinction between nature and habit is crucial because na-ture's operations belong to the nature of the subject, body and soul.[59] If habit is not to be found in the body because bodily ac-tions are natural and not the result of the will, this is true for those actions which are dispositions coming from the nature of the body and not the will. The role of the will in disposing a subject to a habit means that actions involving habit proceed from the soul, that is, the will is the principle of such actions. The sexual nature of the person, the sexual desires and impulses that are present from birth, are natural to the body, and do not concern habit. It is the channelling of what is sexual nature of the body to specific acts

---

56. *ST* 1-2-49.2, *ad* 3.

57. *ST* 1-2-50.1, *resp.*

58. Aristotle, *Nicomachean Ethics*, 2.1.

59. *ST* 1-2-50.1, *resp.*

that are identified with the will and the repetition of the acts forming a habit that involve the will.

Sensitive powers can be considered in two ways, at the level of instinct, the natural powers are ordained to whatever sustains life or preserves the species, while there is the capacity for sensitive powers to obey reason, in this regard, they may have a diversity of objects, all depending on what reason commands whether the disposition is towards good or evil. The capacity to obey reason is indicative of whether habits will be formed. A crucial characteristic of the sensitive appetite is its innate property of being moved by the rational appetite, while at the same time, the rational powers possess an innate quality to be receptive to the sensitive appetite.[60]

A discussion on what constitutes human nature within the framework of habit is revelatory when distinctions are made concerning "nature." We can speak of "specific" nature, that which is common to humans, as well as "individual" nature, that which manifests itself in a specific person. A sexual nature, that is the impulses present which fundamentally serve for the generation of life and the preservation of the human species is present in all humans. Yet, the power of these impulses, these sexual desires that mobilize the person will vary from individual to individual. It seems that Aquinas leaves room to account for the varying differences that would lead to virtue and vice. Bearing in mind that reason and will belong to the nature of the person, it is in this regard that Aquinas can state, "For some are disposed from their own bodily temperament to chastity, or meekness, or such like."[61] It should be clear at this stage that some habits such as those of a sexual kind, can be caused or inclined by one's own nature, while with other habits, this is not the case. The intellective nature of the person may incline one to the habit of rational activity, just as the appetitive nature may incline the person to concupiscible acts.

---

60. Aristotle, *De Anima*, 3.5.
61. *ST* 1-2-51.1, *resp.*

## Single and Repeated Acts

The question that surfaces is how a single act is related to a series of acts that suggest a habit. Reason is the active principle by which the passive one must be overcome, that is, the appetitive one. Reason, however, cannot overcome the appetite just through one act. To be inclined to the same thing like nature belongs to the habit of virtue, rather than a single act.[62] It follows that repeated acts cause a habit to grow. A good habit is what one would call virtue, "Every virtue which an operative habit is, is a good habit, productive of good works."[63] In this respect a distinction can be made between psychological habit and moral habit. Pinckaers points out that for St. Thomas *habitus* requires virtuous acts in order for a *habitus* to be formed; these acts are built on the theological and moral virtues.[64] This formation of virtue can be understood as moral habit. Instead psychological "habit" becomes the repetition of these acts which is what the *habitus* is at a psychological level: repetition, in this sense, "habit." If the individual succumbs to sexual impulses whenever sexual drives are present seeking gratification, the moral act would be considered a vice whenever reason is not engaged in conquering or controlling the appetite. Reason is being repeatedly governed by the sexual appetite in seeking sexual fulfillment, so the existing natural disposition collapses into a habit and a vice.

## Vice and Virtue

Vice and virtue have some resemblances, but they are quite different. If virtue is understood as a disposition towards what is best for the nature of a thing, in other words, a nature that is perfected through virtue, then, vice would be the contrary, something that distorts that nature or brings upon some defect to that nature. It is clear that "nature" is a key principle in what constitutes virtue or using Augustine's definition, "Whatever is lacking for a thing's

62. *ST* 1-2-51.3, *resp.*
63. *ST* 1-2-55.3, *resp.*
64. Pinckaers, *The Sources of Christian Ethics*, 335–36.

natural perfection may be called a vice."[65] Once again reason has a significant role to play because human nature is also what is in accord with right reason; what is specific to the person is the rational soul, and so, what is evil would not be in accord with right reason making such repeated acts a vice.[66] The will is the subject of vice, that is, the person who engages in the repeated sexual act; it is not the object, whether this is pornography, the objectivization of the body, one's own or that of others. The subject of vice is the will of the individual who fails to overcome impulses with a will that governs and controls human sexual activity. The vegetative and sensitive powers of the soul can be moved or restrained by the will, the subject of good and evil moral acts. Even "morose delectation" can be found in reason: (i) individuals may provoke themselves into passionate thoughts of lust; and (ii) although realizing the passionate thoughts are inordinate, they remain unchecked, and the individual continues to dwell on these thoughts rather than attempting to bring them to an end.[67]

Aquinas deals with the problem of reason in relation to the passions raising the question, "Whether reason can be overcome by a passion, against its own knowledge," drawing from Paul's letter to the Romans, "I see that in acting on my body there is a different law which battles against the law in my mind. So I am brought to be a prisoner of that law of sin which lives inside my body."[68] Aristotle's *Ethics* appears to offer a solution when Aristotle states that "knowledge cannot be overcome by passion . . . every virtue is a kind of knowledge and every sin is a kind of ignorance."[69] The will is drawn by a good or an apparent good, and so if the will is moved by an evil, it does so only believing this to be an apparent good which would mean ignorance in reason. Nevertheless, people do act according to the knowledge they have, and the question is, why so?—the claim Paul makes in his letter to the Romans.

65. Augustine, *De Libero Arbitrio*, 3.14.

66. *ST* 1–2–71.2, *resp.*

67. *ST* 1–2–74.6, *resp.*

68. Rom 7:23.

69. Aristotle, *Nicomachean Ethics*, 7.2; *ST* 1–2–77.2, *resp.*

A person in a state of passion may be aware of their moral behavior or the implications of their actions within a given context of distraction or in a situation of opposition or by some kind of "bodily transmutation." A person may be distracted by the power of their passions such that they cannot form a proper judgment of their acts; the force of their passions makes any rational judgment difficult or diminished. As for bodily transmutations, this occurs in a state of sleep or being drunk so the person is not entirely aware of the implications of their moral actions.[70] These distinctions are made because there can be degrees of passions for different reasons. When passions are intense, the person appears to lose their sense of reason.

The use of the will is not only in general knowledge that the person already has, but also in particular knowledge, that is, in reference to the particular act. However, in the latter instance, the passions can lead to obstructing reason, and therefore, the will acts on an erroneous judgment. The capacity of the will can also be weakened by a physically fragile body, the connection that Aquinas makes on the basis of "nature" if a part of the body is not functioning according to its nature, so will the soul, not be able to perform its actions, when the will cannot be ordered by reason.[71] The physically fragile would also include the psychologically fragile.

When a person is affected by the concupiscible appetite the individual's exercise of reason occurs with greater difficulty because of the power of the concupiscible appetite over the will. There is a parallel between the greater the passion due to the fragility of the body, and the greater the weakness of the soul's capacity to carry out an action based on a reasonable judgment. In no terms, however, can the condition of a fragile body be considered the cause of an immoral act or vice, but rather, the will itself, although, the will is affected by the bodily condition. The discussion, then, concerns passions that are very strong and whether the will is diminished, in addition to the voluntary nature of the act. This

70. *ST* 1-2-77.2, *resp.*
71. *ST* 1-2-77.3, *resp.*

is once again connected to the use of reason since the will acts on the basis of what reason presents to the will.

A subtle distinction needs to be made between strong passions due to the state of a person's body as the individual's nature, and thereby, involuntary, and that which is involuntary itself, bringing about the strong passions, but which could have been averted if the activity weakening them had not been pursued. The latter case can be exemplified by a person getting drunk, resulting in the weakened bodily state and reduced capacity to reason. In the first instance, involuntariness is connected to the body itself, such as intense passions, in the second, it is the result of an act that could have been avoided, as in not getting drunk. If an act is considered to be a serious offence, it presupposes that the individual had the capacity to use reason, for reason may be diminished as in a state of passion, but it is never altogether taken away—so a degree of culpability remains.

## Sin

Aquinas reaffirms that what makes acts virtuous is that they are in accordance with nature, and what is in accord with reason is in accord with nature. Instead, vice is contrary to nature, and whatever is in disaccord with reason is in disaccord with nature. In other words, "sin" for Aquinas is a "bad" human act. I also noted the importance of the will for Aquinas, for it is in the will where sin resides.

In terms of desiring a good, Aquinas states that, "Now every sin consists in the desire for some mutable good, for which man has an inordinate desire, and the possession of which gives him inordinate pleasure," so, the ultimate end of the act becomes disordered.[72] One of the characteristics of "fornication" is that fornication not only absorbs the flesh, but it also absorbs the use of reason.

72. ST 1–2–72.2, *resp.*

The virtues that distinguish the acts in relation to God, neighbor and self, is that theological virtues, faith, hope and love, are those in relation to God, justice in relation to neighbor, and temperance and fortitude in relation to the self. Although Aquinas distinguishes the species of these acts, God, neighbor and self, in the case of carnal pleasure, all three vices are implied, lack of theological virtues in relation to God, the absence of justice in relation to one's neighbor, and the failure to show temperance or fortitude in relation to one's self.

Sin itself is disorder in which one departs from God, and from the order of reason. Aquinas makes a crucial point when he states, "Wherefore, as long as any virtuous inclinations remain, it cannot be said that man has the opposite vices or sins." This further suggests that a person can be helped to acquire and deepen this inclination towards virtues such as prudence and temperance. Self-love is divisive, while the love of God, is unitive—the result of vice which divides and virtue that unites. Aquinas claims that "the stronger the impulse to sin, the less grievous the sin."[73] This is a significant moral claim that Aquinas is making which suggests that the greater the impulses, the less the will has control over the person's actions, although reason to guide and inform the will remains present. Sin can also be identified in terms of two causes to sin: (i) direct and proper cause of sin which is fundamentally the will to sin; and (ii) indirect cause of sin, the extrinsic cause where the will is inclined to sin. Aquinas shows the distinction between the direct cause of sin where it is the intention of the will to sin, and the external cause where the voluntariness of the will is diminished.[74] The gravity of sin is also diminished if the concupiscible is understood as a passion and a power in the individual as Aquinas states,

> then a greater concupiscence, forestalling the judgment
> of reason and the movement of the will, diminishes the
> sin, because the man who sins, being stimulated by a

73. *ST* 1-2-73.5, *resp.*
74. *ST* 1-2-73.6, *resp.*

greater concupiscence, falls through a more grievous temptation, wherefore he is less to be blamed.[75]

Sin has a role to play in reason as well in which it may be in reason itself as a result of error: reason may error in the knowledge of truth, reason may fail to check the appetitive powers, and reason may even command the inordinate movements. The external causes of sin inclines the sin to be multiplied in number because of their frequency and repetition. The concupiscible desires are not bad in themselves since they are oriented towards a good such as the need for food and drink and sex, the preservation of life. The inordinate nature of these concupiscible desires are due to inordinate self-love whether this is pride, concupiscence of the flesh or concupiscence of the eyes.[76] Concupiscence of the eyes cannot be subsumed under the concupiscence of the flesh given the role the eyes have in concupiscible desires. The degree of sinfulness in concupiscible acts of the flesh diminishes according to the intensity of the movement of the sensitive appetite which is involuntary, while sin is something which is within "our control" through "reason and the will," and so, in this respect, passion reduces voluntariness.[77]

Two ways in which the will sins of its own accord—where there is the malice of sin: (i) due to a corrupt disposition of the will which may be either due to habit or ignorance; and (ii) in the removal of certain obstacles such as the hope of eternal life or the fear of hell. Aquinas makes a significant distinction between sin committed from malice and sin committed out of passion. He is consistent in this regard associating malice with the will and the intention to sin. Habit also belongs to the category of malice, while passion suggests the diminished capacity of the will.

If we consider original sin in order to better understand the weakened will, the fragile inclinations that lost their original order, we can also see how the human condition remains one that

75. ST 1-2-73.6, *ad* 2.
76. 1 John 2:16.
77. ST 1-2-77.6, *resp.*

is vulnerable.[78] One of the problems caused by original sin is that the will, which was originally oriented towards God, has been disordered in turning against God leading to inordinate powers of the soul. This inordinate tendency means that the soul turns inordinately to mutable goods which is also called "concupiscence."[79] In this section on sin I have drawn from Aquinas to show that the person's free will is never obliterated, even with all the effects of original sin, however, the gravity of the sin may be diminished. While Aquinas recognizes that the person always has the freedom to act according to reason, he also admits that freedom may be affected by the person's condition when dealing with concupiscent desires. The powers of the soul which moves a person's passions reduce the person's capacity to truly act freely since the person also acts in relation to natural desires which are part of the person's nature. Nevertheless, how the will is exercised is distinguished in terms of habit in a disposition to malice, a singular act in which the person recognizes the disordered desire. Due to the concupiscence of the flesh, in the singular act reason still fails to attain an ordered good resulting in sin, however reduced. The individual who develops a particular vice should be capable of correcting themselves by virtue and prayer, to overcome the disordered desires.

## External Principles

In this section I examine the external principles which are those elements that come from outside the individual leading to their choices, and then, how the individual reasons about those choices. These principles range anywhere from a child's upbringing (psychological) as shown in chapters 1 and 2, to the religious influences (spiritual), external principles that I show in the next section.[80]

---

78. It is beyond the scope of this paper to enter into the historical controversies concerning original sin. The Pelagian and Augustinian approaches to Christian morality are discussed in my paper, "Christian Morality: Pelagius and St. Augustine," 67–82.

79. *ST*, 1–2–30.4, *resp.*

80. Religion can function at various levels, psychological (culpability often

These experiences of the individual, whether at the unconscious or conscious level, may create anything from a neurotic condition due to a rigid legalism to developing a sense of freedom by making the most virtuous choices.

In order to live in union with the will of God, so that the individual may be truly happy in pursuit of the ultimate Good, two approaches to morality have been given with two different traditions: (i) one is based on commandments, a series of rules, of what to do and not to do, and with this the reward and punishment that is attached, also known as "voluntarism"; and (ii) an approach that is based on desire, to be with God and the desire of beatitude, properly speaking, "liberty." Thomas Aquinas's approach to morality is expressed in the freedom of interior desire to be united with God.

## End and Finality

For Thomas Aquinas the individual can have multiple ends and multiple forms, with partial and intermediate ends as well—however, these ends are relative to an ultimate end the perfect good of the person which finds its perfect accomplishment perfectly satisfying the intellectual appetite, and such an end can only be one.[81] The morality of an act is the result of a subject who is oriented from the interior where there is no external force imposed upon the individual, towards an end known and loved—the morality is measured in relation to the morality of the end.[82] All goods that attract the intellectual appetite do so only in relation to this ultimate end.[83]

Aquinas resolves the difficulty of the human end in its extra-subjective character, and the possession of the good, so that, there

associated with the superego), social (family and society impose given norms of behavior), and spiritual where a person acts for an ultimate good or even out of fear.

81. *ST* 1-2-1.5, *resp.*
82. Plé, *Vie Affective*, 36.
83. *ST* 1-2-1.6, *resp.*

are not two different ends, but one end, the good itself, and the possession of the good. The two cannot be dissociated, they act from one reality: they constitute one metaphysical unity. The distinction, thus far, can be made between the sensitive appetite which seeks a particular good, and the intellective appetite which seeks a universal good, or one might say, "good" and "Good," respectively.[84] The significance of a particular good that brings delight is that because it is in reference to a universal good, which is the true good being sought, Aquinas avoids the problem of a hedonistic ethic. The crucial point is that pleasure is not suppressed in Aquinas's ethics, but rather, pleasure has a determined place, and as joy, it is the end of all human acts.

All things that are desirable can be said to be good and is an end for the appetite. Distinctions can be made between what is useful, pleasing and honest: useful is understood as that which is desired as a means; something that is pleasing is that which brings the appetite of the subject to a repose and tranquility; and finally, the honest is that thing which is the final and ultimate end of the intellective appetite.[85] Human acts put some kind of order in an internal harmonization of the human tendencies, each playing a role in harmony with all the others exercising a common finality relating the subject to something other which is ultimately God. Each human operation has its finality, such as the eye, with the view to see, so, together the senses are ordered towards intelligence, and finally, the entire human being which is ordered to an external reality, namely, the enjoyment of God. This accounts for human acts being unifying and also integrating. With each appetite desiring

84. *ST* 1–2–4.2, *ad* 2.

85. *ST* 1–5.6, *resp, ad* 2. The term "honesty" is problematic in English because "honesty" has a narrowed definition pertaining to truth. John is an "honest" man because he is truthful, a law-abiding citizen. However, by extension and the sense intended by Aquinas, if John is an "honest" man, this reflects his moral conduct—his overall behavior sheds light on his values, those of an honest person, a person with moral integrity, and this moral integrity is manifested in the outward person, a sign of what is inside, a kind of external and internal beauty. This is the notion of Aquinas's *honestas*: a moral beauty. On the significance of *honestas* see Pinckaers, *The Sources of Christian Ethics*, 391, 415–17.

the good which suits the appetite, the senses seeking pleasure, the will must bring the senses to a superior and ultimate good that permits the inferior appetite, while exercising its dynamism, to surpass itself.

Honesty is not a thing desirable in itself even though honesty is desirable. That which is sought is intrinsic goodness, for that which is within it, being itself, "For a thing is said to be honest as having a certain excellence deserving of honour on account of its spiritual beauty: while it is said to be pleasing, as bringing rest to desire, and useful, as referred to something else."[86] This means that the honest good is that which the intellective appetite is attracted to, while the pleasant good, is that to which the sensitive appetite is attracted. This suggests that the moral act has two dimensions in reference to the object whereby goodness and beauty coincide: the moral act is the love of an honest good. Love of an honest good can be qualified as love of friendship, using Aristotle's definition, "to love is to want something good for someone," and this reference is only to a person, while for things, such love is a love of concupiscence.[87] A friendship that is utilitarian or delectable is not a true friendship.[88] This key assertion shows that a true friendship does not use a friend for utilitarian or purposes of pleasure, but rather, the friendship is the result of the goodness of the person. It is the person who is loved with all their qualities and shortcomings, and such love of friendship is reciprocal.

## Meaning of Law

For Aquinas the law is the "principle" of human acts because the law serves as their "rule and measure," and the object of human acts is happiness.[89] The law, therefore, needs to be understood in relation to happiness. Since the individual is part of a community,

---

86. *ST* 2-2-145.3, *resp.*

87. Aristotle, *Nicomachean Ethics*, 8.2.

88. Aristotle, *Nicomachean Ethics*, 8.4.

89. *ST* 1-2-90.2, *resp.*

the law is also intended to serve the common good which itself is aimed towards "universal happiness."[90] But Aquinas also points out that the law should have an efficacious power to induce virtue in the person.[91]

It might appear that the obligation to obey is a precept that opposes freedom. If the one who puts the precept into practice acts out of love, and not out of fear, then, the person acts freely. The precept of love can only be observed by a personal choice and so it is not opposed to freedom. Evangelical love is truly love that is free. Aquinas maintains that the will freely desires while it desires necessarily, a continuation of Augustine's position that liberty opposes the necessity of constraint, but it does not oppose natural necessity.[92]

The notion of "constraint" is a crucial one since it directly pertains to freedom—a person who is constrained to perform an act is said not to be free, and so, the act cannot be considered as having moral value. Constraint in a human act is not natural, and so constraint is to be opposed to that which is natural in a human act. Everything that corresponds to an interior law, that is, a person who is moved from within, is said to be natural. Similarly, the inclination, as well as the act that comes from the subject, is said to be voluntary—in the pursuit of what is good.[93]

## Divine Grace

Whether in the pre-fallen or fallen state, the person is in the need of God's grace, but for different reasons. In the pre-fallen state,

---

90. "The end," "the law" and the "common good" are interrelated in terms of the external principles presented in this section. This relationship with the "common good" is also expressed in the other two external principles (following), "grace" and "love." I do not develop Aquinas's moral anthropology in relation to the community in detail.

91. *ST* 1-2-90.3, *ad* 2.

92. For details on the Augustinian discussion on freedom and necessity in relation to freewill see my work, *Amor Dei*, chapter 2.

93. *ST* 1-2-6.1, *resp.*

grace is needed to perform or desire anything that is good. In the state of integrity the person could perform or desire goodness in proportion with human nature as in acquired virtue, but not surpassing human nature, as in infused virtue.[94] In the fallen state, grace is needed because the individual is incapacitated to attain any goodness due to sin, although the natural endowments of the person can perform some limited particular good. Grace enables the person to purify, to reinforce and to raise this openness towards God, and grace has a moral value also because it restores and animates human freedom. This shows that it is not the will that orders human acts, but rather, reason itself, since the will tends towards the good according to reason. The appetite of the intelligence is the universal good. It is in the good that the will finds its finality, and this finality known and wanted is what gives the human act the quality of being moral.[95] Thus, grace is needed in the post-fallen state on two accounts: first, in order to be healed, and second, to carry out a good act.

## Quality of Love

The understanding of "love" as a friendship shows that love contains benevolent quality, that is, a person wishes good for the other.[96] If this benevolence is not present, that is, a love that is not self-interested, then, the love is one of concupiscence, where the person is treating the object of love as a possession to be used.

In Aquinas's moral anthropology the human act is a moral one or a reasonable "love" in so far as the act is motivated by the love of an object known and judged by the intelligence. The role reason plays in human affectivity is what distinguishes human and animal affectivity, where in the former case it is said to be spiritual, and in the latter, it is said to be sensorial. This shows that human intelligence by knowing and desiring, and then moving towards

94. *ST* 1–2–109.2, *resp.*
95. *ST* 1–2–1.1, *resp, ad* 2.
96. *ST* 2–2–23.1, *resp.*

or wanting the object, can have an affective life that is proper to it, and not only a sensorial affectivity as one finds with lower animals. This also means that if an act is either arbitrary or constrained, where there is no will present, there is no moral act. The moral act as an act of love is based on freedom and love.[97] This is brought out clearly in St. John's Gospel, "If you love me, you will keep my commandments."[98]

Love as a result of the intellective appetite, that is, a love that is reflected and reasoned, is the most noble form of human love as created in the image of God. The moral end is also a love of delectation producing a sense of attraction in the person and awaking and exalting a complaisance within the person, an affinity which leads to some form of union whether in the form of friendship or in the expression of conjugal love. These aspects of attraction from complaisance to union express the movement out of the person, love as ecstatic.[99]

In this chapter I have presented Aquinas's moral anthropology in order to provide a framework to evaluate sexually addictive behavior. The different elements accompanying the moral anthropology of the subject has been presented, as well as their relations. I have looked at the relationship between the passions and the moral act. I have also shown the crucial role played by reason in directing the will in determining the moral act. Since the will is always present in human acts, even if its capacity is diminished due to the will's wounded nature, neither internal nor external principles obliterate the will. I have also looked at the significance of habit and disposition in the acquisition of virtuous behavior. Nevertheless, the central role of the will in its diminished capacity requires pastoral considerations in counseling and accompanying a person with behavior that is sexually compulsive. The sexual acting out is not a collapse of the will, but an ongoing realization of the struggle confronting the individual with addiction.

97. *ST* 2-2-19.4, *resp.*
98. John 14:15.
99. *ST* 1-2-28.3, *resp.*

# 4

# Examining Pleasure

In this chapter I will look at sexual acts in relation to pleasure and the ambiguity of pleasure due to the wounded state of human nature since the Fall. This chapter further explores how pleasure is to be morally interpreted: the underlying moral considerations in determining the freedom of the will; and the relationship between addiction and pleasure. These considerations will also show the intersection between counseling and spiritual support for individuals who experience sexual addiction.

## Good, Pleasure and Happiness

Human experience shows that a person is naturally inclined towards a good because this good appears to be the source of happiness. This means that as far as the person wills, the person is principle of their own "free-will" and is therefore master of the acts that accompany the "faculty of will and reason."[1] The difficulty lies in that there are a multiplicity of goods and many of them appear to bring happiness, when, in fact, none truly satisfies the human will, unlike the Blessed in heaven who have perfect hap-

1. *ST* 1–2–1.1, *resp.*

piness possessing perfect freedom with their will totally placed towards the supreme Good. The freedom to choose is the result of the intelligence and the will enlightening the individual, which goods should be pursued, in reference to the Supreme good. The "freewill" is the common act of reason and the will.

Human freedom is not the result of either the number of objects from which a person can choose, nor from indifference, but out of love—acting out of love is when one acts out of freewill, whether this is acting out of love or out of pleasure, as Aquinas maintains.[2] Reason places order in the will which is an order of truth allowing reason to tend towards an object. An object that is known by reason, can be objectively attained by the will, that is, in its truth. At the same time, without this objective truth the act is neither human nor moral.

Human acts cannot be separated from the Creator, either, because God, even if confusedly, is the object of all knowledge and love.[3] The human limits of the person, the desire-to-be and the desire-to-live, presented in finite forms, are based on a radicality of desire even deeper than being and life for itself, so that these concrete forms are never fully satisfying, as in the absolutizing experience of pleasure. A distinction can be made between the finite forms of concrete and limited experience, and the universal desire of the infinite, the pleasure of desire being fulfilled without limits. The person loves something that surpasses being itself, something absolute that is attached to human desire. This means that the human act leads to God, and as a result, it can be said that it is God who permits the human act and invites the individual to pose human acts. God calls from the inside to want freely and from the outside to love through the objects of knowledge and the intellective appetite.

2. *ST* 1–2–1.5, *resp.*
3. *ST* 1–60.5, *resp.*

## Bodily/Non-bodily Pleasure

Experiencing pleasure from one's thoughts, of course, is not the same as experiencing a sensory pleasure; the sensory experience of pleasure is greater in intensity than one's thoughts of pleasure which is why corporeal experience is often sought in itself.[4] Nonsensory, that is, spiritual pleasures, require a person of virtue because sensory pleasures are more easily and more widely known, while spiritual pleasures are the delights of the intellective soul. Furthermore, the bodily experience of sensory pleasures also serve as a remedy for "sorrow and sadness."[5] These views that Aquinas presents are supported by case studies where sexually compulsive behavior functions "to medicate" pain from the past. Individuals who have a passionate temperament and are always in need of some remedy for their passions, their bodies "searching" to satisfy their intense needs, because pleasure removes pain, any kind of pleasure, provided that the pleasure is strong, is why passionate individuals tend to fall victim of vice and intemperance. Aristotle illustrates this by comparing the person who is in good health, and who has good sense of taste, can also recognize the sweetness or temperature of food, while the ill person will have distorted tastes.[6] At the moral level, an upright person would be able to identify what is right and just, while a person who is morally deteriorating would not reject immoral pleasures because of failing to identify them, not unlike an ill person who cannot taste something sweet or warm. Instead, for the virtuous person, activities bringing pleasure are those that perfect the individual, such as contemplation.

Aquinas acknowledges intellectual pleasures as associated with the will, a spiritual affection, which he refers to as *gaudium*, "joy." The other kinds of pleasure that cover both the spiritual and the sensory are known as *delectatio*.[7] Aquinas maintains that all beings are in potentiality and find their achievement in act, and in

---

4. *ST* 1–2–31.5, *resp, ad.* 1.

5. *ST* 1–2–31.5, *ad* 1.

6. Aristotle, *Nicomachean Ethics*, 10.5.

7. *ST* 1–2–31.3, 6.

this actualization finds its good, and the "en-joyment" of this good. The act is a *quietatio*, a "stillness," that brings rest, a stop to the movement and a satisfaction to desire. Pleasure as an immanent act of the subject is fulfilled through an object, thereby, finding the subject's own perfection. By the possession of the object, the subject finds itself enriched by this love, because the object suits the subject for its actual needs.[8] Pleasure is not possible without the object that is loved that produces this pleasure; an affective union between subject and object, the subject needs to be conscious of this union. This explains why beings without knowledge cannot experience pleasure.[9]

## Experience of Touch

One of the dominant sensory experiences in relation to pleasure is that of "touch" which needs some consideration because of the nature of this particular sense. It would appear that the pleasure of "touch" is the greatest sense that can be experienced.[10] Although sight is regarded as pleasure in the sense that it gives knowledge, pleasure refers to the reason of usefulness which is "touch." This means that the pleasure of touch is far greater than the pleasure of sight because of the usefulness of the former.[11] The animal nature is shown in sensory experience, "for dogs do not take delight in the smell of hares, but in eating them."[12] The pleasure of natural concupiscence is aimed towards nutrition and sexual union, for example involving the intensity of tactile experience.[13] A pleasure is not natural when it is not in accordance with either human nature or with reason.[14] That which is common to humans and animals are forms of pleasure that involve food, drink, and sexual activity.

8. *ST* 1-2-34.1, *resp.*

9. Aristotle, *Nicomachean Ethics*, 10.5.

10. Aristotle, *Nicomachean Ethics*, 3.10.

11. *ST* 1-2-31.6, *resp.*

12. Aristotle, *Nicomachean Ethics*, 3.10.

13. *ST* 1-2-31.6, *ad* 3.

14. *ST* 1-2-31.7, *resp.*

There may be some things that are co-natural to the individual when the nature is corrupted but is not natural to the species, and this corruption can be of two types, either coming from the body, or coming from the soul.[15]

## Possessing What Is Craved

The other question that is addressed is whether pleasure causes thirst or desire in itself.[16] Since pleasure is an emotion of the appetite of something present, the craving for the thing means that it is not possessed or not entirely possessed. However, pleasure does suggest the presence of a thing craved for. This defective presence may be due to either the possessing subject or the possessed object, as when possession of the object is not entirely whole, but possessed in sequence, taking pleasure of more and more of what remains. In the case of the possessor, this is the possession of a thing in parts over time. An individual can also become tired of repeated bodily pleasures and may seek other forms of bodily pleasures. Pleasure may also exist in the imagination or as a memory when a pleasure was experienced in the past and pleasures are imagined.

### Morality of Pleasure

Pleasure is understood as the perfection of the finality of an act—pleasure is the object of desire. One may ask whether the basis of the moral act is the good or pleasure, especially because the good is in view of the pleasure that it brings.[17] Since pleasure is perceived as a good, it is desired, and therefore, perceived as an end. It would seem then that pleasure is the ultimate finality in the person; but, if that is the case, then, this would lead to an epicurean eudemonism

15. *ST* 1–2–31.7, *resp.*
16. *ST* 1–2–33.2, *resp.*
17. Aristotle, *Nicomachean Ethics*, 10.4–5.

or a hedonistic ethics, neither of which Aristotle espouses, nor Thomas Aquinas.

## Intentionality of the Act

Aquinas makes a distinction between spiritual pleasure and sensory pleasure, that is, the pleasure that is derived from the spiritual appetite, and the other that derives from the sensory appetite. These distinctions fall also within the difference between animal pleasure and human pleasure: the animal without capacity to reason remains at the level of the sensory appetite, while humans are capable of reason capture the general idea of the good through sensory pleasure, that is, reason has a role in transcending the particular experience seeking something of a universal, so that the Good is sought rather than pleasure itself.[18] The experience of pleasure itself cannot be given a moral attribute as good or evil, but the conformity of pleasure with its finality, like any of the natural appetites, thirst, hunger, sex.

## Considering Circumstance

The moral implications—the "circumstance"—in relation to a moral action also needs consideration. Circumstance is treated as "accidents" to a moral species, just as a person who has a substantial nature, also has accidents as part of that nature.[19] An individual who visits a friend for a social evening and is unexpectedly exposed to pornography or provocative sexual advances, is not the same as someone who searches for pornography or searches for a sexual liaison. In addition to reason that determines the object specifying the moral act, the circumstances of the act is the principle condition in which the act occurs. Circumstance has a bearing on the moral weight of the act.

18. *ST* 1-2-4.2, *ad* 2.
19. *ST* 1-2-18.3, *resp.*

## Basis of Consent

One does not choose from necessity because it is possible also not to choose, and this is based on the power of reason: any single good can be chosen or can be avoided if it lacks the good and has some aspect of evil. The related problem to acting out of necessity, is freedom of consent. The individual who is drawn to a good and adheres to reason may consent as part of the appetitive power, moving towards the desired object, or the apprehensive power, affirming that the object is a true good to be pursued.[20]

The word *con-sentire* "to feel with" expresses the idea of consent, and since this is a movement towards the object, consent is an act of the will used in reference to those things present: the imagination has the capacity to recognize what an object is like, even in the absence of the actual object, while the intelligence itself can apprehend universal ideas in the absence of particulars. In the case of the appetitive power, the appetite inclines the individual to the thing itself, and attaching the person to the object through these powers, the person is said to have a kind of "likeness" to it, a kind of "sense" of the thing. In this way, the person comes to know the object directly by also taking some "delight" in it; this delight is also known as "complacency." Aquinas ascertains that consent is an act of the appetitive power, although consent is, technically speaking, part of the apprehensive power. As far as "likeness" is concerned, in the sense of seeking similitude, the person is inclined to the object cleaving to it and for this reason consent is in the appetitive power.[21]

## Obstructing Reason

There are three ways in which bodily pleasures may obstruct reason: (i) by detracting from reason when one's attention is focussed on an object of pleasure; (ii) in some cases pleasure is contrary to reason as a result of pleasures that are in access; and (iii) in some

20. *ST* 1-2-15.1, *resp.*
21. *ST* 1-2-15.1, *ad* 2.

instances bodily pleasures lead to an alteration in the body and so reason is effected.[22] The significant point here is that bodily pleasure does not find repose until it is united with the object of pleasure which means some alteration of the body in attaining both a tranquil state of body and soul. With the bodily alteration, the acts may be contrary to reason.[23]

Pleasure as perfecting an operation of the soul needs to be closely examined as well. Considering Aristotle's assertion, that "pleasure perfects an operation" this claim can be broken down into two further assertions: (i) when a good that completes a thing, thereby, adding to an operation, there is rest as an end, and in this sense, perfects it; and (ii) as a subject (agent) so that pleasure is not some kind of an object, but proper to the agent itself, and thereby, increasing activities leading to pleasure and diminishing those that do not.[24] The distinction between rational pleasures and bodily pleasures suggest that pleasure arising out of reason strengthens the faculty of reason, while those that arise out of concupiscence diminish reason—concupiscible pleasures seek concupiscible pleasure.[25]

The sensitive appetite may be part of an instinctive experience as much as it may be part of a spiritual experience—in both instances, experienced through the body. Significantly, Aquinas avoids compartmentalizing the body to separate acts: the spiritual, sensory and vegetative appetites cannot be separated in the human individual, but rather, human acts are a substantial union of these three faculties. Aquinas's ethics builds on his metaphysics: the person experiences as a being, composed of matter and form, body and soul, so, pleasure cannot be an end in itself. However, by misusing the body, sexual pleasure becomes an end in itself. The problem of sexual addiction is precisely this sort of opposition

---

22. Aristotle, *Nicomachean Ethics*, 10.5.

23. *ST* 1-2-33.3, *ad* 1.

24. Aristotle, *Nicomachean Ethics*, 10.4–5.

25. *ST* 1-2-33.4, *ad*. 1.

between body and soul: corporality becomes a source of pleasure, and is used for pleasure.[26]

## Human Sexuality in God's Creation

Considering the creation of man and woman in the image of the Divine, Aquinas has always emphasized that this imaging refers to human intelligence and freedom. That which refers to the rational domain is what distinguishes humans from other animals, as seen in chapter 3. Aquinas maintains that the sexual character of humans is associated with the reproduction, but the sexual act does not reflect the divine image; for Aquinas his moral anthropology places the sexual act within a reproductive finality.

A radical difference existed in the intellect and the will in relation to the passions in the pre-fallen and fallen states.[27] The account in Genesis 1:27–31 is the pre-fallen state where God's rational creatures were in harmony with God, with the other and with themselves. The object of their desires was not pleasure, but communion, and communion would have been experienced through sexual pleasure. The passions in the pre-fallen state were not an instrument of pleasure but of communion, and they were entirely under the command of reason. The disordered state after the fall weakened the use of reason, and heightened the passions, and as a result, were vulnerable to having disordered sexual pleasure as an object, thereby, objectifying and instrumentalizing the body.

The creation of man and woman highlights the goodness of the creative act because it is in God's "image and likeness" that they are created, and God emphasizes in the case of the human creature that "indeed it was very good." The goodness of this creation

---

26. I presented autobiographical elements of Sue Silverman's sexual addiction which shows precisely this instrumentalizing of the body which for her was a "fix" for something missing—"love." One of the individuals whom I have counseled refers to different forms of sex as "medicating" the body. In such sexual experiences the body is treated as matter, separated from spirit.

27. *ST* 1–95.2, *resp, ad* 1.

76

with the mandate to be "fruitful and multiply" reflects the ordered goodness of the divine act.[28] Human sexuality in the order of creation, and the original state, is also something good.

This original divine order in which humans were at harmony with God, with nature and with themselves, collapses after a rupture with the Divine Creator.[29] The passage from Genesis presents the disordered state specifically in relation between the man and the woman, this suggests something of the sexual order: both man and woman are subjected to suffering in their disordered state, the labor the man experiences and the woman at labor, both associated with dis-pleasure. But this suffering caused by the rupture with God, exists at several levels, and not just one in which human sexuality has lost purpose "be fruitful and multiply," but harmony has been replaced with "domination."

With the collapsed order, the sexual appetite along with human nature is radically weakened, and human nature will remain in a fragile state reflecting sexual disorder. As shown in natural order and disorder, before and after the fall, respectively, moral theology, and the underlying anthropology, needs to take into account precisely the human condition before and after the fall. This pre- and fallen state represent a radical difference, between rational creatures in harmony with God and creation, and a disharmony due to a grave act of disobedience. This means that because of the prevailing disorder, human sexual desires, and pleasure in fulfilling these desires, are not good in themselves, although this was the case when there was natural harmony. Rather, the goodness of human sexual acts and pleasure are determined by the object of sexual acts, that is, the intention of the act.

## Sin and the Human Condition

Sexuality is also the domain where one experiences the guilt associated with the Christian experience of temptation and separation

28. Gen 1:26–31.
29. Gen 3:11–17.

from God. In this rupture the individual affirms him/her-self against God, as Saint Augustine maintains, in the perverse imitation of the Divine.[30] Perverse because the individual attempts to subvert the established order by God, re-introducing a new order, a human order, thereby, also subverting the authority of God.

Salvation from sin is offered by Jesus Christ who was crucified, died and rose from the dead for the sins of humanity.[31] The Christian is asked to pursue this salvific path by following Christ in obedience which means death to one's sins and to oneself. What is radical in Christianity is not only the salvation offered through the person of Christ, but the moral intensity of sin causing the profound rupture with God, humanity and the individual. Harmony in the natural order first disrupted because of human sin, with God, with oneself, and in relation to others, is the sign of sin's radicality.[32] Sin has spread not only in relation to God, and between man and woman and in their unequal relationship of dominance and power, but now between men, fratricide's ugliness spreading into the world. Sin spreads in global proportions, and God reacts.[33] In a god-like fashion society attempts to reach God using their own talents, their own strength, power and ambition, as if to rival God.[34] The spread of sin, this fallen human state, cannot be dismissed, and any moral theology that is built needs to take the "wrecked" human condition into consideration, in order to re-order one's self to a life of virtue and good habits, with the help of God's grace.

## Pleasure and Reason

The role of pleasure needs to be understood in relation to reason, and a nature that has been wounded by original sin. Human

30. Gen 3:5; Augustine, *Confessions*, 2.6.

31. 1 Cor 15:3–4.

32. Gen 4:8.

33. Gen 4:11–13.

34. Gen 11:4.

pleasure is not just the objective acquisition or possession of a desired object, but the subjective experience of this object. It is important to note that these two ends, in fact, constitute one, "acquisition" and "enjoyment." This is also true for the moral end of the individual which is ultimately the Good, the reality of an honest good, the act which this motivates, and the pleasure that accompanies the act.[35] The implications for human activity are significant: if there is pleasure associated with the activity there is a greater intensity—awareness—of the act which gives growth to the individual leading to a greater desire to contemplate and to learn, this also leads to greater perseverance in the activity.[36] Similarly, the Good is sought because of the pleasure the good brings and that one finds, while one avoids evil because of the sadness that evil brings.[37] This means that pleasure is not a bad thing, but rather, something good within moral activity. The pleasure one experiences with the individual one loves intensifies the love, and this is also true for the Good leading one to seek and attain the Good.

Pleasure is the reality of human experience, and yet, pleasure cannot have its own finality, not sexual pleasure as Aquinas presents the concupiscible to us. Sexual pleasure has as a finality procreation. An anthropology that creates a dichotomy between body and spirit separates sexual pleasure from its unitive and procreative finality, thereby, reducing pleasure to a hedonistic ethics; a person cannot be helped to recover from sexual addiction if pleasure is pursued for the sake of pleasure, as a finality in itself. We have seen in case studies, and studies in psychoanalysis, that early childhood experiences may serve to either trigger or exacerbate sexually neurotic behavior in the form of sexual addiction. These considerations are part of a counseling and spiritual support process in finding ways to help a sexual addict to recover from addiction and live a more psychologically, emotionally and spiritually integrated life.

35. Plé, *Vie Affective*, 101–2.

36. Aristotle, *Nicomachean Ethics*, 10.5.

37. *ST* 1–2–59.3, *resp.*

## Consequences of the Fall

Pleasure is part of the dynamism of the moral act, provided that it is properly ordered. Actions are considered morally good so long as the end is in conformity with the reasonable nature of the person.[38] For Aquinas the experience of pleasure was far more intense before the Fall than the children of Adam and Eve. The question of sexual pleasure during coitus is brought to Aquinas, and he replies,

> Beasts are without reason. In this way man becomes, as it were, like them in coition, because he cannot moderate concupiscence. In the state of innocence nothing of this kind would have happened that was not regulated by reason, not because delight of sense was less, as some say (rather indeed would sensible delight have been the greater in proportion to the greater purity of nature and the greater sensibility of the body), but because the force of concupiscence would not have so inordinately thrown itself into such pleasure, being curbed by reason, whose place it is not to lessen sensual pleasure, but to prevent the force of concupiscence from cleaving to it immoderately. By "immoderately" I mean going beyond the bounds of reason, as a sober person does not take less pleasure in food taken in moderation than the glutton, but his concupiscence lingers less in such pleasures. This is what Augustine means by the words quoted, which do not exclude intensity of pleasure from the state of innocence, but ardour of desire and restlessness of the mind. Therefore continence would not have been praiseworthy in the state of innocence, whereas it is praiseworthy in our present state, not because it removes fecundity, but because it excludes inordinate desire. In that state fecundity would have been without lust.[39]

The effects of original sin create a wounded pleasure; lust which was not part of sexual pleasure in God's original plan, has now become a strong inclination in the sexual act. This is because the human will has been weakened due to original sin, making

38. *ST* 1–2–34.1, *resp.*

39. *ST* 1–98.2, *ad* 3.

sexual desire vulnerable to lust.[40] The result is that the human dimension of pleasure, as was experienced before the Fall, has now been diminished since the intelligence is needed to humanize pleasure. The human experience in coitus resembles more that of animals because of the concupiscence that is heightened and the diminished presence of reason. The position maintained by Aquinas is not one of intensity of pleasure that ought to be sought, but rather, the participation of the interior appetite in the experience of pleasure.

## Consent to Sin

Passions can be the principle of human acts with the participation of the will in the sensible powers. Humans share with animals this sensitive appetite, and in animals, objects perceived through sensory knowledge move towards the object with a determination and necessity without any free judgment, unlike in the person, where this sensitive movement participates in something of freedom. It should be noted that for Aquinas there is no mortal sin due to sensuality since for a sin to be good or evil, the act must be ordered to an end known to be good or evil and sensuality in itself is incapable of doing this.[41] Sin involving the passions is only possible when reason orders the will to want the satisfaction of this movement. Three elements are involved as Aquinas states,

> the internal cause of sin is both the will, as completing the sinful act, and the reason, as lacking the due rule, and the appetite, as inclining to sin. Accordingly something external might be a cause of sin in three ways, either by moving the will itself immediately, or by moving the reason, or by moving the sensitive appetite . . . something external can be a cause moving to sin, but not so as to be a sufficient cause thereof: and the will alone is the sufficient completive cause of sin being accomplished.[42]

40. *ST* 1-2-82.3, *resp.*
41. *ST* 1-2-74.4, *resp.*
42. *ST* 1-2-75.3, *resp.*

The appetite may incline to sin by restraining reason or the intelligence, but in this case, with the appetite restraining the will and/or reason, the human act is imperfect, and proof for the imperfection of this human act is that the will does not take delight in the act, instead, it is saddened by these acts to which it has not fully consented, when it has been restrained by the sensitive appetite.

Sins caused by passion have the element of regret and remorse associated with the act, while someone who sins by freewill takes delight even in having sinned.[43] Participation of the will in the sensitive appetite is proper to humans; in addition to the memory which is also present, making human acts cogitative. The highest degree of the will in the sensible appetite is to be found in temperance and force, when the concupiscible participates in the appetite without conflict, the principle of human acts rationally becomes virtues.

## Lust and Pleasure

Lust is the mind's preoccupation with sexual pleasure. Sexual addiction has "lust" as a motivating cause, although, deep-seated in the lust itself can be psychological layers which have been explored in the first two chapters of my work. Between the unconscious psychosexual dynamics, and the sexual acting out, lust is at work and therefore requires some consideration.

The question may be asked what is the object of lust, or what does lust seek? St. Thomas maintains that lust pertains specifically to sexual pleasure, but the real problem has to do with excess, and as a result, "creates havoc in man's mind."[44] There is no doubt that Aquinas associates the sexual act with an end which is good, that is, procreation, and as long as the Commandments of God are observed as well as right reason, there is no lust of the flesh in these acts.[45] Based on Aquinas's thought, three conditions can be

43. *ST* 1-2-78.4, *resp.*

44. The following sections on lust are taken from *ST* 2-2, qq. 153–54. See also Vogt, *The Freedom to Love*, 98–103.

45. *ST* 2-2-153.2, *resp.*

set when an act is one of lust: (i) an access of sexual pleasure associated with the imagination; (ii) when sexual pleasure does not conform to right reason; and (iii) when sexual pleasure is not in conformity with its end which is procreation. The importance of Aquinas's position is that sexual pleasure is not contrary to the natural law, nor to Divine law when it conforms to reason, and to its natural end. Two individuals who are not married engaging in the sexual act does not conform to right reason because they are not taking into account the good of the children.[46] The nature of lust as a sin is due to excess, not the sexual pleasure. The significance of this assertion is that the act of sexual pleasure does not have sin attached to it provided the sexual act is ordered by reason. The result of lust is that the natural appetite (lower powers) dominate in such a way, so, the acts are disordered along with the higher powers, that is, reason itself.[47] Aquinas breaks the sexual act governed by lust into four parts: (i) the failure to apprehend something as a good because it is hindered by lust; (ii) right council as a result is impeded by lust; (iii) this is also true for the act of judgment, governed by lust; and (iv) the reason's command about the thing to be done is also impeded by lust since the act is governed by lust and not what reason orders the individual to do.[48]

46. That is when the act does not go against right reason, right morals or the Commandments of God, *ST* 2–2–153.2, *resp;* 154.2, *resp.* There are three goods to marriage, procreation, the couple, and the children. This moves into the discussion of premarital sex which is not the purpose of my work. My work is not about the sexual act whatever that act may be, it is about sexual addiction, and so, the focus remains on matters that have addiction as the core problem in human sexuality. "Quantity," the repetition of the act is not the issue, either, since this may occur legitimately within a marriage. It is when the act fails to engage in its natural end, and has the pleasure of the sexual act as the end, which for Aquinas goes against reason, and in this case, would be considered "lust."

47. *ST* 2–2–153.5, *resp.*

48. Also, Aristotle, *Nicomachean Ethics*, 6.5, where intemperance corrupts prudence which is the fundamental flaw one finds with "lust," excess meaning intemperance, and the person, therefore, fails to act prudently.

## Divisions of Lust

For Aquinas lust can be divided into six "species": (i) fornication; (ii) adultery; (iii) incest; (iv) seduction; (v) rape; and (vi) unnatural vice. In these categories the relation "due" to the other expresses the offence of lust. In other words, lust violates justice in the form of some bodily possession. Sexual addiction concerns lust as far as excess is concerned, and not the species, as Aquinas presents them.[49] Although excess refers to something quantified, where two individuals are concerned, one does not see this as being for the good of the marriage, so, the sexual activity is not by mutual consent, since this would be sinning to be with one's own spouse inordinately. The basis of dividing lust into six distinct species is based on seeking sexual pleasure without the use of right reason. Clearly, the role of the intelligence has a central role in determining whether lust is present or not in two particular ways: a) obstructing procreation which is the vice against nature; and b) the good of the children due to fornication.[50]

Lust following Aristotle's interpretation of "vice" is best defined, therefore, in terms of excess.

## Unnatural Vice

The question of unnatural vice as a species of lust is most pertinent to the discussion of sexual addiction since Aquinas, thus far, has argued to show that there are six species to lust, with unnatural vice being the sixth one. "Unnatural" may be understood in terms of excess in addition to the power of sexual desire and pleasure that motivate lust, leading to inordinate forms of sexual pleasure. In chapter 2 I gave a re-interpretation of sexual addiction based on "repeated sexual acts," "out-of-control behavior" and "consequences" that the individual comes to recognize as part of their sexual patterns. Unnatural vice would belong to such categories since the sexual addict governed by lust, finds an endless cycle of

49. *ST* 2–2–154.1, *resp.*
50. *ST* 2–2–154.1, *resp.*

sexual fantasizing/imaging (lust) only to be followed by sexual satisfaction (acting out), returning to the previous state of fantasizing/imaging (lust). Some of the characteristics of unnatural vice is that it is a non-generative or a non-procreative act; something "unbecoming" of the sexual act that makes it unnatural, and that is, non-procreative in character. This does not mean unnatural vice equals sexual addiction, but may trigger addiction since they are separated from their finality, which is procreation. Lust is contrary to right reason and unnatural vice is contrary to the natural order. This "unnatural vice" manifests itself in several forms: (i) "procuring emission [orgasm] without copulation"—these are masturbatory acts that seek sexual pleasure; (ii) copulation with something that is referred to as "bestiality"; (iii) same sex relations with reference to Rom 1:27; (iv) unnatural form of copulation (oral/anal sex).[51] Sexual addiction is driven by repeated acts inducing pleasure obtained by one or more of these unnatural vices. The affirmation concerning lust is that sexual pleasure is sought not procreation which is what makes lust unnatural.[52]

In chapter 4 I examined pleasure in relation to both happiness and sin, since pleasure is connected to both. From the different kinds of pleasure from bodily to non-bodily, I also presented the different contexts in which pleasure is experienced, as well as the freedom to consent and factors that may obstruct reason. Finally, I considered the implications of the human condition, that of sin, and how the will has been affected in the fallen state from pleasure to lust.

---

51. *ST* 2-2-154.11, *resp.*

52. It should be noted that for Aquinas the category of unnatural vices due to lust are considered the most offensive because they do not conform right reason, failing to act according to the person's nature. These vices are, therefore, doubly serious: (i) because they are lustful; and (ii) because they go against nature. See, *ST* 2-2-153.12, *resp.* In terms of gravity, Aquinas maintains that it is not the omission of the proper use, but rather, the abuse, so, the sin of omission of copulation with another (masturbation) is the least offensive, compared to bestiality which is the worst, due to the abuse, the proper use of the species not being observed; same sex relations follows that of bestiality where the right sex is not observed; and finally, not observing the proper manner of copulation.

# 5

# Elements for a Moral Evaluation
# and Means of Support

In chapter 3 I presented St. Thomas's moral anthropology as a foundation to evaluating human actions, and in chapter 4, I focused on the ethical stakes involved in pleasure. I began by considering human nature itself in the Thomist tradition, and central to this discussion is human reason, the will and the last end.[1] The human faculties were considered with close attention paid to concupiscence, the passions and the imagination. The role of both reason and the will, working together, or acting in conflict, becomes apparent in these different faculties where concupiscence, the passions and the imagination are present. I also examined the internal and external principles in moral activity. In the case of the internal principles, the significance of habit and disposition was underlined, with further development on virtue, vice and sin. In terms of the external principles, the discussion considered in particular the function of the law and grace. The focus of chapter 4 was pleasure, the different types of pleasure, and the relationship between pleasure and morality. Furthermore, in chapter 4 sin and

1. Chapter 3.

the human condition were examined, especially in relation to St. Thomas's question on "lust."[2]

In the present chapter I re-examine the different kinds of sexual addiction that have been the focus of my work in the light of the framework provided. The chapter serves a twofold purpose. First, this section gives the basis of a moral reflection and possible evaluation of sexually addictive behavior. A moral evaluation of the acts and conduct of an individual with reference to psychoanalysis shows the underlying unconscious factors that may be at work in the addict's compulsive sexual behavior affecting the will. Second, I suggest possible means of spiritual/pastoral support, as the sexually obsessive individual recognizes this fragile state, and seeks to overcome the sexual addiction.[3] In this last section, I consider avenues of psychological support for the addict, besides a spiritual framework for pastoral care with the hope of the addict's spiritual, emotional and affective integration.

## Moral Evaluation

To give a moral evaluation of the sexually addictive acts and behavior of an individual I have shown the signs of sexual addiction, subsuming them into three categories, as well as the different factors that may lead to sexual addiction.[4] These range from the psychosexual development within a Freudian framework, precocious sexual experiences and sexual abuse, to shame in morally rigid homes. These varying factors need to be taken into consideration in any moral evaluation of the acts of the person. Moreover, the nature of the sexual addiction also needs to be weighed in

---

2. Chapter 4.

3. I wish to emphasize that in offering care to the sexual addict that my interest is of a spiritual nature, hence, my emphasis will be on spiritual care. This does not exclude other avenues of support; on the contrary, spiritual care considers the entire person, and the other forms of support that are available, therapeutic and group support.

4. See chapters 1 and 2 above for details.

determining the moral implications of the act. I will re-examine the types of addictions that were presented in chapter 2.

## Pornographic Addiction

Sexually obsessive behavior that involves pornography may appear to be the least harmful morally since this only involves the viewer, either flipping through pages of a magazine, or more widespread surfing pornographic sites on the internet. There are three questions that can be asked: (i) Why is the viewer addicted? (cause); (ii) What is involved with this addictive activity? (moral); and (iii) What are the moral consequences of the act? (effect). If pornographic addiction is due to narcissistic tendencies emerging in the early-stages of psychosexual development, or if compulsive pornographic viewing becomes an escape from the experiences of childhood "shame," the moral gravity of these sexual acts is reduced since we are dealing with early psychic "layers" of material that are being somehow triggered.[5]

I showed in chapter 2, that pornography does not satisfy pleasure, it serves to create the need for pleasure to be satisfied. The aim of the addict is pleasure, and pornography becomes a means of attaining this goal. The habitual nature of addiction where the person feels they no longer have control over their actions, suggests a degree of powerlessness in the will, although reason serves to inform the addict of the consequential aspect of the behavior. At the relational level the individual consuming pornography

5. Pornography was covered in chapter 2. An example comes from an eight-year-old boy in a southern Italian village who installed a video game into his computer. The program produced sexually explicit sexual advertising that neither he nor his parents were able to remove. The problem of children inadvertently being exposed to pornography may become another risk in pornography addiction. See Harris, *Cognitive Psychology*, 296; and Greenfield, "Inadvertent Exposure," 741–50. A Finkelhor et al., study shows that one out of four youth 10 to 17 years old have the internet experience of unwanted exposure to naked people or people having sex (*Online Victimization*, 50). For psychosexual development see chapter 1, above; for neurotic tendencies, "shame" and "ego-defense mechanisms" see chapter 2, including sections on pornography.

becomes progressively more self-withdrawn and isolated, viewing sexual activity in instrumental terms—a means to pleasure. While pornography in itself does not bring satisfaction, it anticipates satisfaction, an outlet, some kind of release. Pornography becomes, therefore, a catalyst to increased sexual activity, first viewing sexual images, and second, need for sexual satisfaction. The power of consent is diminished, while the need to succumb to sexual satisfaction is increased; the weakened will fails to co-operate with reason. The pleasure anticipated, and the habitual nature of the act, reduces the moral weight of the action.[6] The culpability of the addict is taking the initial steps with viewing pornography in mind, knowing the outcome. The initial movement towards the pornography is where the gravity of moral responsibility is increased. G. Cucci observes that withdrawal in terms of studies, concentration, social activities and becoming more sexually preoccupied may already occur in pre-adolescence much in the ignorance of the parents in how the youth spends his/her time.[7] Ultimately, parents play an important role in identifying the causes of the addiction and seeking therapeutic support for prevention and healing.[8]

## Masturbation Addiction

The previous section shows that pornography normally follows with sexual activity to satisfy the sexual needs created by the pornographic material. As I have indicated, pornography is followed by masturbation or some other sexual activity creating sexual release.[9] Nevertheless, masturbation is not necessarily preceded by pornography. A sexually compulsive person may have sexual desires provoked by a whole series of visual factors in addition to the addict's own imagination. In this regard, it morally does make a difference when the individual seeks to fuel the imagination with

---

6. *ST* 1-2-77.7, *resp.*

7. Cucci, *Dipendenza Sessuale Online*, 40–41.

8. Cucci, *Dipendenza Sessuale Online*, 41.

9. See chapters 1 and 2 above.

pornography choosing in advance to reduce the will's power, with increasing sexual desire caused by the pornography. A compulsive masturbator who does not turn to pornography has already shown some virtue by attempting to keep the will in check. Already, the moral gravity of the masturbator is reduced because some means are taken to act virtuously, force and prudence being two of the virtues the addict has already exercised in advance. The compulsive masturbation may be the result of factors discussed above, where masturbation is triggered by underlying psychosexual factors, surfacing in defense mechanisms.[10] These underlying factors, in Freudian psychosexual development, the family attitude towards sexuality, precocious or abusive sexual experiences, may be factors leading to compulsive masturbation. If this is the case, there is something in the person's concupisible "nature" that would incline the individual or predispose the individual towards compulsive sexual behavior, and therefore, weakening the person's culpability due to the will's weakened position.[11] As with pornography, masturbation suggests a progressive withdrawal of the individual in relational terms, and becoming increasingly isolated serves to heighten the addiction.

## Cybersex Addiction

Sexually compulsive behavior that makes use of the internet for cybersex is a combination of two distinct moral acts, and potentially a third: (i) going online with the intent of sexual activity; (ii) engaging a person in sexual activity; and (iii) increasing the possibility of physical sexual activity.[12] While in cybersex no physical contact takes place between the individuals, making this appear morally less grave, nevertheless, cybersex has the relational implications that another person is involved, either enticed, or succumbed, into masturbatory sexual acts.

10. See chapters 1 and 2 above.

11. *ST* 1–2–77.3, *resp.*

12. See chapter 2 above for details.

The relational dimension of cybersex where another person is involved increases the gravity of the sexual act since another human being is led, or one is being led by another person into masturbatory sex. Cybersex, whether with a stranger or with a friend, increases the risk of engaging physically in sex, and so, the person continues to fuel their sexual addiction in cybersex. While pornography leads to masturbation, cybersex involves masturbation, but potentially leads to physical sexual encounters. A moral evaluation of cybersex means if a person is not on-line viewing pornography, s/he is engaged in a relational experience, possibly anonymous, albeit, with no physical contact. In this case, human interaction places greater responsibility on the individuals involved since they can choose to "disconnect" from the encounter, although, once again, the will's force diminishes as the sexual acts are viewed. This is why the lack of prudence in cybersex, as with pornography, is the principle fault; the initial viewing followed by increased sexual desire creates a need for sexual gratification which is achieved through masturbatory acts. In order to morally evaluate cybersex, the question for moral reflection is whether a person who is sexually fragile is capable of acting prudently? To be prudent is to look ahead and foresee uncertainties; prudence is to discern that which helps or hinders the individual in reaching God.[13] It would appear that the nature of habit and prudence become increasingly mutually exclusive terms: a person engages in sexually compulsive behavior, because there is a failure to act with prudence. This inability to exercise prudence among cybersex addicts is a fundamental part of the moral problem, and can be attributed, as we have seen, to unconscious psychosexual factors stemming anywhere from infancy to adolescence.

A sexually compulsive individual who seeks sexual fulfillment may not consider prudence as an option, since the objective is pleasure. The fact that sexual pleasure is sought through a combination of online sources leading to cybersex, with a high possibility of physical encounters, suggests once again an escape

---

13. *ST* 2-2-47.1, *resp, ad* 1 (in reference to St. Augustine).

mechanism to find "medication" through sexual pleasure.[14] Yet, with these different means through which sexual pleasure is sought, failing to act prudently knowing their fragile condition, the addict's culpability increases, although, this is not to say that the addict has complete control over their sexual acts, and may account for their inability to exercise prudence. Cybersex shows that in the absence of a relational experience, the individual engages in "anonymous" cybersex without any kind of self-giving, or commitment to the other, reflecting another form of self-withdrawal.

## Multiple Sexual Partners Addiction

Sexual addiction that has escalated to multiple sexual partners can have a variety of causes, and a proper moral evaluation would need to consider the underlying factors: psychosexual development, attitude towards sexuality in the home, possibility of sexual abuse, early sexual experiences whether this is with masturbation or sexual intercourse. In chapter 1 an example was provided of a case where marriage was seen as a solution to pornography and masturbation addiction. Instead, the marriage led to other sexual partners, both opposite sex and same sex. The sexual addict needs to address the underlying cause leading to sexual addiction. This underlying cause also has moral implications. Sue Silverman reveals how her sexual addiction was caused by sexual abuse as a child, and her multiple sexual partners seen as an attempt to "medicate" this abuse. With such underlying psychosexual considerations, a person's moral responsibility is reduced, and the gravity of sexual acts are reduced.[15] Nevertheless, serious moral problems remain with multiple sexual partners because they involve a series of sexual contacts, whether friends, bath houses, cruising streets and parks, picking up prostitutes, fitness centers or bookshops. In each instance a conscious choice is made to seek an individual for sexual gratification, and to entice a person into engaging in sex.

14. The need of "medication" has a variety of causes, from childhood shame to sexual abuse.

15. *ST* 1–2–77.2, *resp.*

## Further Considerations

Pinckaers maintains that, "every person possesses basic moral inclinations and a primal moral sense that no corruption due to sin can completely destroy . . ."[16] Fundamental to the premoral act is the role of freedom: for the human act to be a moral one, it must occur freely, not with force or out of ignorance. The premoral act, as Pinckaers points out, is one based on natural inclinations that have human nature as the basic principle of morality. If the premoral act is one based on such inclinations, that is, one which is perceived as good because of the individual's moral condition, this raises difficulty in sexual addiction, since addictive behavior suggests an inclination towards actions which the person perceives as necessary, and overpowers reason. As Aquinas shows for an act to be moral, there must be an exercise of the will, in pursuing a good, but also in avoiding evil. This is, precisely the problem in the premoral act, one is at the level of inclinations as the perceived good.

An observation that Albert Plé makes, relying on Freudian psychoanalysis, is that unlike the freedom that engages the individual in a moral act, at an unconscious level or prehuman level is "more frequent in human conduct than acts that are properly human."[17] This prehuman level that motivates the person to act, is where unconscious material is stored from infancy, and remains present, although not consciously accessible.[18] This suggests that human acts may be triggered at a prehuman level which could also help explain why the sexual addict is morally weakened reducing the responsibility for the compulsive sexual activity. These prehuman acts structured by early life experiences cannot be ignored in giving a moral evaluation of the sexually addictive behavior.

---

16. Pinckaers, *The Sources of Christian Ethics*, 357.

17. Plé, *Vie Affective*, 115 (my translation).

18. See the next section where the prehuman is further developed based on Plé's research. The analogy of rock formation in geology that Plé uses provides a wonderful illustration of the unconscious where material remains present, and further material is added to and/or formed upon the earlier material. See also Freud, *Civilization and Its Discontents*, 15–19.

## Deep-Level Conflicts

In this section, drawing especially from Albert Plé, my aim is to show how "deep-level" conflicts may manifest themselves at a surface level in terms of compulsive sexual behavior. My focus in this "deep level," as Plé asserts, reflects the early stages of psychosexual development of the individual which may manifest itself later in life in different forms of sexually addictive behavior. By attempting to identify the potential area of conflict, especially in terms of how pleasure is understood and experienced, especially in sexual pleasure, I will be able to consider paths for the suggested care. I will look at conflicts of pleasure, the external laws governing pleasure, and finally, the body-spirit conflict.

## Some Conflictual Elements on the Nature of Sexuality

One of the factors triggering conflict is the human experience between sexual activity and guilt feeling manifested in "power"—this is symbolized especially by the male sexual organs.[19] While sexuality is only one dimension of the person, other significant considerations include religion, and ethnicity, but as noted in chapter 1, sex has a crucial role to play touching the core, the very being of the individual. "Sex" is a category employed to identify the person— the way masculinity/femininity is defined by the complementarity and opposition. Freud showed the fundamental role that sexual differences had in the psychosexual structure of the male and female.[20] "Castration anxiety" is the area where the differences between male and female become most apparent: in the case of the

19. The collapse into a pagan practice of worshipping a golden bull in Exod 32:4 expresses the recognition of male virility, power, wealth. The new religious observance for which the Israelites were chastised is not only at some conscious level, but at the unconscious level manifesting what is fundamental in human instincts: the need to survive. A Platonic interpretation of this would be the desire for immortality, as shown in Plato, *Symposium* 206e–207a in *The Collected Dialogues of Plato*.

20. I presented Freudian psychoanalysis in chapter 1 as well as certain objections.

female the anxiety caused by the loss of the penis, while in the case of the male, there is ongoing fear of its loss, and in both instances, the result is anxiety. The phallus, as symbol of power, has the same significance for the boy and girl: to have or not to have a phallus which further means that the phallus constitutes a fundamental part of the child's self-image: possessing or losing the phallus questions one's self-identity.[21]

The conflictual nature of castration anxiety is reinforced by the Oedipal complex in which the child seeks to unconsciously eliminate the parent of the same sex, since that parent possesses the desired object, the parent of the opposite sex. Tension manifests itself because as much as an unconscious desire remains present to eliminate the parent, the child would also lose the love on which the child depends eliminating the same sex parent. As a result, these unconscious desires are both that which bring life (desiring the parent of the opposite sex), but also that which brings death (eliminating the parent of the same sex).

This situates sexuality within anxiety and the fear of death; the death wish shows that the fulfillment of Oedipal desires are life and death, that which must be followed with the pain of not being oneself and being oneself with what is forbidden. The Oedipal conflict means that one is obstructed from being oneself: the realization of oneself is confronted with the interdiction caused by the Oedipal conflict, and as a result, a false identity: identifying oneself with the rival that one seeks to eliminate. A moral evaluation of sexual addiction is not just an assessment of what the person is doing, or failing to do, but understanding what is taking place at a deeper level—the root of the addiction, the mechanisms and conflicts that are operative, and whose expressions appear at a surface level.

---

21. Laplanche and Pontalis, *Vocabulaire de la Psychanalyse*, 74–75.

## Interior/External Laws

Albert Plé's criticism concerning relation between moral conduct and the law is based on an "external law"—a moralizing attitude towards human sexuality.[22] The external law imposed from the outside is compared to the Freudian *superego* which not only governs the *id*, but imposes itself from the outside, leading to conflict, and a neurotic sexuality. External laws may be experienced in the form of a puritanical rigidity that serves especially to create a sense of shame and guilt.[23] Plé's position is that the *id* which is continuously battling with the *superego*, the external laws will begin to repress if not block sexual desires, leading to an unhealthy and neurotic sexual disposition.[24] Carnes showed in his case studies that children often experienced sexual morals in what he described as "rigid" homes where sexuality was associated with shame and guilt experiences. Bradshaw found the same patterns in sexual addicts, when "shame" is one of the most dominant features of their perception of sexuality, leading to sexual addiction pattern as an attempt to free themselves from the imposing laws. In this respect, sexual acts are the result of suppression, the *superego* suppressing the libido's drives, surfacing in unrestrained sexual acts.

Home environments that are excessively rule-governed with laws being imposed to observe a moral code run the risk of collapsing into addiction because of the suppressed sexual desires, or associating sexual desires and the need for sexual expression as "bad." If the child is socialized in this moralizing environment that is harmfully rigid, the sexual addiction that results has been structured by oppressive conditions in which the child has no outlet, and later suffers the consequences of these conditions as an adult. As I show in the next section, a support for such individuals needs to re-examine human sexuality as well as the child's past, to help re-discover both the sexual and spiritual in harmony rather than in conflict. Since the conditions of the addict may be retraced to

22. Plé, *Vie Affective*, 11–13.

23. Shame and guilt were dealt with in chapter 2 above.

24. Plé, *Vie Affective*, 13, 124.

a psychosexual structure in early childhood sexual development, these initial layers that remain present and operate at the unconscious level, resurface as a neurotic condition in the sexual addict.

As sexual desires take powerful expression among adolescents, it is not the preoccupation of sins against the flesh that should shape adolescent morality, but rather, moving towards maturity and that only a positive outlook on chastity can resolve without some kind of psychological trauma.[25] The adolescent is confronted with the moral law that may appear beyond human capacity, and when these moral demands are externally imposed, they risk being rejected, leading to compulsive masturbatory practices without defined limits or needs. Aquinas's sense of what is natural means discovering of human sexuality as a gift from God, but a gift serves a purpose, in sexual identity, in the powerful desires of loving, and, the sexuality of procreation.[26] The obsessive sexual practices leads the adolescent to the absolutizing of pleasure, and a predisposition to addiction since external laws run the risk of creating the need for an outlet, psychological, sexual or otherwise.

While an unhealthy rigidity in imposing external moral codes may contribute to sexual addiction in a context where the child is vulnerable, totally depending on the values within the home, external laws cannot be entirely dismissed as they serve as a point of reference in the sexual maturation when the interior freedom to make proper choices, striving for virtue simply fails. There may be a "collapse" in those virtues, different forms of obstruction due to the individual's own psychological state at a moment in time, and so external laws cannot be outright rejected. Although obedience to external laws may suggest voluntarism as opposed to a life of

---

25. Plé, *Vie Affective*, 13. Plé argues that the superego has a similar function to that of externally imposing laws on the adolescent. The topic of "chastity" is treated below.

26. The relationship between sexual pleasure and procreation has been consistently maintained by Natural Law theorists. See, *ST* 1-2-31.7; Finnis, "Law, Morality, and 'Sexual Orientation,'" 1049–76, at 1067. Grizer, *The Way of the Lord Jesus,* 651. The fact that a person is a sexual addict does not change the nature of human sexuality as expressed by these authors, nor does being an addict dismiss the addiction as morally acceptable behavior.

Beatitude, this external obedience is used to bring the person out of a premoral state where inclinations as desires are pursued as a good, without the proper rational reflection, to a morality that evolves from freely made choices based on virtue. In other words external laws or "barriers" may serve as a pedagogical tool in early states of moral development while avoiding the extreme of rigidity.

## Antinomies: Body and Spirit

Given Freud's psychoanalysis the person's need for sexual gratification is at the premoral level, while the tension due to the Oedipal conflict and the antinomies of happiness and pleasure are at an anthropological level. Christianity places the believer in relation to God, and God in relation to the believer in terms of promises and their fulfillment, and sin in relation to their redemption. If sin is the fundamental obstacle to redemption due to the rupture with God sin causes, the imitation to be God is *perversa imatio Dei*.[27] It is Jesus Christ who saves the individual sinner, sin that has a twofold gravity: (i) deprives the individual from the fulfillment of the promise and is destined to death; (ii) at the same time sin usurps the only one who can fulfill the promise, God. The sexual addict operates in a state of denial, the denial that any sacrifices are needed, or pleasures to forgo, until the sexual addict begins seeking spiritual help. Only at this later stage, does the addict expressing that s/he has not given up on God, nor has God been denied or the participation in divine life.[28]

## Suggested Paths of Care

There is a two-pronged approach to recovery, that is, to overcome sexual addiction by continued support and guidance, so that the individual becomes progressively integrated spiritually,

27. Gen 3:5.

28. At what point the sexual addict moves from denial to admission and what causes this "change" is a question that should be further studied.

emotionally and sexually. First, psychological support which I approach from the perspective of therapy (psychoanalysis, cognitive . . .) to determine unresolved underlying areas that are a factor in the addiction, and account for the obstacles in recovery, and concretely change behavior. The second is the spiritual care that the person receives through spiritual counseling, meditating the Scriptures, reception of the Sacraments, especially the Eucharist and Reconciliation, as well as the re-integration into a faith community. The latter form of support is intended to help the Christian find both guidance and nourishment in Christian teaching. The Scriptures offer hope in Christ, and the Sacraments that are the means of overcoming human weakness, whereby the individual is given the spiritual means to acquire the virtue that is needed in working through addiction.[29]

## Psychological Support[30]

In this section, I will show the significance of psychological support, that is, what practical steps may be taken to support and help a sexual addict towards increased abstinence.

An example I will use is from an individual who sees me for spiritual counseling and has given me reasons why he needs psychological support at the same time as spiritual. He recognizes that at the root of his addiction there are early childhood experiences at the age of four or five years old that he remembers through a process of "target memory" in his therapy. Immediately associated with childhood memories of seeing a naked woman in the shower room, was being scolded by his mother for his extended stares. His first experience, therefore, was the shame he felt for looking at a

---

29. The use of "two-pronged" as an expression was employed by a counselee telling me the advantages, he found using these two approaches rather than just one.

30. A link provided by a counselee contains material directed towards moral growth and spiritual care, http://theporneffect.com/ This link is intended to help Christian youth live a chaste life. Also, the Chastity Project: https://chastity.com.

woman's naked body. This sense of guilt which followed marked him and later experiences when he was six or seven years old involving pornography, repeated the earlier event, one of shame and guilt, but added to this, there was excitement, "secrecy" and "defiance." These feelings did not change as he entered puberty, at twelve years old he began downloading pornography, and masturbating by the time he was thirteen years old on a daily basis, and more than once a day. It was not until he began university studies at seventeen years old that he recognized he was a sexual addict. His therapist who uses Eye Movement Desensitization Reprocessing (EMDR) therapy helps him return to these earlier memories of feeling shame and guilt, and trying to re-visit them in a positive light, so the feeling of shame, guilt and being "bad" can be understood differently.

Moral counseling is specifically needed to show why the sexual addict is not a "bad" person, while, the addictive cycle needs to be rejected, as causing upheaval in the life of the addict. At the same time help from a therapist serves to give the addict a positive evaluation of him-/herself, while helping the individual identify sexual areas that trigger sexually compulsive behavior. In this respect, we can see how the spiritual counseling and the therapy resonate together.

This therapy is further supported with visits to Sex Addicts Anonymous, where a group of addicts offer each other support, and where a buddy system enables them to talk to each other whenever they feel they are about to "act out." One of the main points this individual reaffirmed was that "he could not do this alone." These meetings help to discover there is "no shame," "no guilt," "no judgment," in talking about themselves and their addiction. The whole point of having this support system is recognizing the need for others, and this includes the need for God. The network of support, both spiritual and psychological, are fundamental in the recovery process.[31]

---

31. See my article, "Treating Sexual Addiction," 1–16.

## Freudian Approach

As Freud asserts, pleasure confronts the principle of reality, the world itself means that pleasure seeks to gratify and obtain, but also to avoid suffering.[32] The addict uses sexual pleasure to deal with suffering; having sex is a way of dealing with past wounds, as strategies of escape, a form of covering wounds, when healing is being sought by engaging in sex. The immediacy of pleasure is where the sexual addict expresses both need and weakness, since pleasure is sought, at all cost, and right away. A move towards temperance and healthier forms of pleasure would be part of a support program by providing other means of fulfilling pleasures as opposed to ones that are addictions. The job of the psychoanalyst is to help the patient overcome the need for immediate pleasure. This is also true for the narcissistic tendencies of the individual failing to make a transition from fundamental auto-erotic needs to a more unitive expression, that is, a failure to move outside from oneself due to the narcissistic investment in the object.[33]

Infancy expressions of auto-eroticization, masturbation and other forms of sexual pleasure are forms of narcissism and when fixated the individual fails to grow out of the phase. The therapist accompanying the person would have to lead them outside a self-focused and self-absorbed sense of pleasure and move to something more creative, more social, more spiritual. Sexual maturity means moving away from the subject and an object of narcissistic interest to the principle of reality, integrating the person by moving beyond sexual pleasure and sexual union that transcends the infantile auto-erotic libido.[34] The integration of the person at a sexual level, as well as the emotional and spiritual levels would be the objective of the therapist. A "fix" which is common in the language of the sex addict, or to "medicate," are ways in which sexual addiction becomes a tranquilizer, so that pleasure becomes closed in itself, as if pleasure is sufficient in itself, when it leads to only more

---

32. Freud, "Formulations," 18.

33. Freud, "Pour Introduire au Narcissisme," 81–105.

34. Plé, *Par Devoir ou par Plaisir*, 176.

desire.[35] The need to re-discover other forms of pleasure as well, as sexuality that is not narcissistic, requires guiding the sex addict to healthier view of human sexuality as well as the expression of pleasure, and at the same time developing strategies forming relationships to escape narcissistic tendencies. The individual needs to recover from that which causes the anxiety, the suffering and the narcissistic solutions of an obsessive self-absorbed sexuality, by moving outwards, into an external expression of gratification and fulfillment, where pleasure does not mean sexual, but the multi-layered richness of varying possibilities of non-sexual expression and pleasure.

## Paths of Relational Support

I have considered four areas of sexual addiction, often inter-related, as in cybersex making use of on-line pornography and chat lines, and then, multiple sexual partners. Some sexually compulsive practices are inseparable as in pornography that follows with masturbation. This means that the support that is needed reflects the kind of sexual addiction that is involved. A sexual addict who compulsively masturbates may need to spend more time in relation with others, a path that leads to the development of interpersonal skills, establishing emotionally healthy relations built on mutual trust and shared interests, and moving away from activities, especially isolated ones, that could trigger sexual imaging. The other extreme is the person engaged in multiple sexual partners; this individual does not have difficulty with creating interpersonal relationships, but rather the problem of sexualizing these relationships. In this case, group meetings and encounters, such as those used by Sexual Addicts Anonymous and Sexaholics Anonymous offer a good starting point, since these members can talk to each other with their difficulties in an open and transparent manner and building new relationships. From pornography to multiple sexual partners, these suggested paths of support require time for

35. The term "a fix" was also used by a counselee.

encouraging results. There is success in abstinence/sobriety, and then there is failure in "acting out." These patterns may go on for years, but these paths of support, inter-relational skills and group therapy, should not be discontinued because of a relapse.

## Spiritual Care

In terms of spiritual support discovering God's love is a foundation to any form of counseling. God's love is a call to God, but also a call to conversion, knowing God from personal experience. The call is to enter into relationship with God, and not just to learn about becoming virtuous (Deut 6:4).[36] God's call is expressed in the passionate words of Isaiah, "Come back to me, for I have redeemed you" (Isa 44:22). God's call is not only a call to return, but a reminder that God has redeemed us. In Saint Paul's letter to the Romans, this unquestionable love that Christ has for the individual is a source of reassurance and comfort that regardless of one's sins, Christ still loves the sinner, ". . . nor any created thing whatever, will be able to come between us and the love of God, known to us in Christ Jesus our Lord" (Rom 8:39). St. Augustine's journey of conversion expresses well in his *Confessions* the depth of God's love, seeking and calling the individual,

> Thou calledst and criedst unto me, yea thou even breakedst open my deafness: though discoveredst thy beams and shinedst unto me, and didst chase away my blindness: thou didst most fragrantly blow upon me, and I drew in my breath and I pant after thee . . .[37]

36. It should be noted that loving God is a command and not a matter of choice (Deut 6:4). This is echoed in Matthew's Gospel, love as a commandment (Matt 22:37–38). Similarly, in John's Gospel, loving God is to "obey" his commandments (John 14:15). This command to love is considered "interior," from within. This obedience means listening attentively with heart, soul, mind and strength.

37. Augustine, *Confessions*, 10.27.

In terms of spiritual support the addict needs to develop a sense of self-love which is different from narcissistic love.[38] Self-love invests energy in the subject while proper love moves outwards towards the object in an ecstatic love. The point of departure, therefore, for the sexual addict is a proper, and ordered "understanding" of love and "experience" which begins with a recognition of God's love for the sexual addict, then a properly ordered self-love, and finally, a true love for others. These three expressions of love are inseparable although they are experienced in different phases of the recovery process of the sexual addict.

## Conversion

This "command" to love God is a command that implies "obedience" as St. John Gospel states, "If you keep my commandments, you will remain in my love."[39] The paradoxical imperative of obeying a commandment, and love which is a free act, seems to be in conflict, as shown in chapter 3 within Aquinas's moral anthropology. From a psychological perspective Antoine Vergote makes an important observation, "The one who loves moves his center of gravity towards the existence of the other, while preserving this center in himself."[40] By the very nature of love, there is a shift taking place, a movement outwards towards the other, while the person does not lose the center of gravity. This push outwards, the result of love, is this law, a movement taking place, the same law of love, the command one is asked to observe. Vergote adds, "The person who consciously assumes the spontaneity of love obeys that which love requires to express itself in truth."[41] This call of God means that authentic love, turning to God, requires conversion; the commandment to love God is the law of love which is an imperative to love God. The conversion to God also means to

38. See Pinckaers, *The Sources of Christian Ethics,* 42–43 on the distinction of self-love and narcissistic love.

39. John 15:10, 12.

40. Vergote, *"Tu aimeras,"* 169 (my translation).

41. Vergote, *"Tu aimeras,"* 169.

renounce that which holds one back from God, conversion and renunciation go together by exercising virtue. A person becomes truly human when chaotic and disordered passionate impulses are renounced and re-ordered by virtue and grace because such impulses are known to be destructive. Love implies the renunciation of egocentric and "oniric" desires because there is never a pure agapetic love, so that the giving and renunciation are integral parts of human love.[42] Since self-interested love is in human nature, that is, some kind of personal benefit is sought in relationships, a person loves because they feel loved in return, so, the egocentric character of love is overcome through some kind of self-giving and self-sacrifice. Grace is the supernatural assistance that raises human love to an agapetic level.

## Divine Assistance

With God's help it is possible to overcome sin and to live righteously.[43] A message of hope is to be found in the Scriptures whereby the sexual addict can be re-assured that there is not only forgiveness, but also freedom to be found in Christ, "through his blood we gain our freedom, the forgiveness of our sins."[44] The first movement towards recovery is this divine assistance, God's grace, that leads the individual to the freedom offered through Christ, his blood, a free gift, for the forgiveness of sin. The sex addict seeks help because the individual recognizes there is something "out-of-control" with their sexual habits leading to personal disintegration. This freedom is offered by Christ, as St. Paul states in Romans, "Christ set us free, so that we should remain free. Stand firm, then, and do not let yourselves be fastened again to the yoke of slavery."[45] St. Paul shows that sin is like slavery, but Christ frees the person like a

---

42. Vergote, "*Tu aimeras*," 171.
43. *ST* 1–2–109.9, *resp.*
44. Eph 1:6.
45. Gal 5:1.

liberator from slavery, ultimately from sin. This freedom offered by Christ is the process of liberation for the sexual addict.

The sexual addict experiences at a personal and inter-personal level a rupture in three: rupture with the self, a rupture with others, and a rupture with God. Reassurance is needed that Christ loves them and there is hope for them to become free individuals. Recovery begins from recognizing that God loves them, that from this love they can learn to love themselves, and they can move outward to an ordered love of others, and through the reaffirming and reassuring love of others, they can recognize their love for God.

---

GOD

Self        Other(s)

←→

---

The pleasure of having found God leads a person to the first steps of a life inhabited by grace.[46]

## Temperance

Aquinas describes "temperance" as a virtue that inclines the person to the good by the use of reason. While temperance is in accordance with the rational nature, it is not in accordance with the animal nature that "is not subject to reason."[47] The virtue of temperance cannot be perfect if it fails to respect obedience and worship of God, this is why paths of support begin by placing the sexual addict in the presence of God.[48] The virtues of temperance and chastity work together so the individual may gradually re-discover sexual sobriety. Temperance has as its material object

---

46. *ST* 1–2–112.5, *resp*.

47. *ST* 2–2–141.1, *resp, ad* 2.

48. Plé, *Vie Affective*, 168. Sex Addicts Anonymous as with any twelve-step program recognizes as a first principle the "powerlessness" of the addict, which leads to the second principle, dependency on God.

food, drink and sex.[49] For the addict, temperance may be a first step in any kind of progress. Someone who has moved from daily pornography to weekly pornography is making moral progress, even if the addict is still masturbating daily. As far as exposure to pornographic images, the addict is making progress in being more chaste. Chastity and temperance are interconnected virtues since chastity involves a "curbing" of the flesh, which is done with the help of temperance.

Sex is a pleasure that involves primarily touch, which then prepares to sharpen the persons desire and need for satisfaction. Modern technology is effective in creating sexual desires, from photography to the internet which capitalize on the visual to create the need for satisfaction. Even if neither visual nor tactile is present, as I showed in chapter 1 and chapter 4 on "lust," the imagination is highly effective in triggering sexual desires. If the addict is repeating the addiction in a ritualistic fashion, temperance can begin by disrupting the ritual, so that, the sexual acts are themselves reduced. Temperance is the basic virtue that moderates human passions; those which are natural, and those most affected by original sin, passions of the concupiscible such as love, desire, sex and pleasure, are the most difficult to order.[50]

If the moral issue at stake concerning sexual acts is really the narcissism of their sexual acts, then the person needs to be gradually introduced to the experience of self-giving love.[51] This may first be discovered with the spiritual counselor working with the addict, in what is a gratuitous relationship of guidance and support on the part of the counselor as the addict receives spiritual support. The moral anthropology elaborated in chapter 3 suggests that the person who has progressively withdrawn from family and friends, and who mistakenly finds healing and medication through compulsive sexual practices, needs to be led to healthy relations.[52]

49. *ST* 2-2-141.4, *resp.*

50. *ST* 2-2-141.3, *resp, ad* 3.

51. Plé, *Vie Affective*, 147. In chapter 2 I indicated that psychology studies on sexual addicts describe the behavior as having narcissistic tendencies.

52. See Cucci, *Dipendenza Sessuale Online*, 40–41.

Re-discovering family relations and friendships that have been abandoned can help the addict as a way for re-directing focus and energy on relations that integrate positive experiences. The sexual addict needs to be understood not as an intemperate person who has morally disintegrated—something that the addict feels and is aware of when help is being sought—but someone who is fundamentally seeking love, a love that was displaced or distorted leading to the sexual addiction. The failure of the person's integration due to a destabilizing past, manifests itself in neurotic conditions. This rupture is noticeable in struggling with virtue that continuously allows the inferior powers to dominate and annihilate the superior ones in a form of narcissistic regression. This rupture that the addict experiences between reason and the will, can be overcome with an ongoing re-examination of one's personal journey, discovering the gratuity of love through renewed relationships, moving from an inward self-obsession and sexual compulsion, to an outward expression of new possibilities, from the relational to the artistic.

Sexual passions have a power of their own and resist reason as a result of original sin. Imposing external laws on the passions may cause further resistance, and although "laws" are needed at first for the addict, the goal is to replace these laws with a reasonable participation for the good and integrity of the person.[53] When the sexual passions are overpowering, they may need to be calmed at first through some use of force of the will by taking concrete actions as to avoid succumbing to one's weaknesses.[54] For instance, installing a SonicWall on a computer; not visiting areas that are a cause of temptation; and putting aside unhealthy friendships. However, this is only to allow a more positive management of the passions. Both are involved in this case, rejecting disordered passions and then moderating them; it is proper to the virtue of temperance in moderating the passions. Resistance to moderating the passions suggests a duality, an internal conflict where the person is torn between two forces, not unlike St. Paul in his letter to the

---

53. *ST* 2–2–141.1, *resp.*

54. *ST* 2–2–151.3, *ad* 2.

Romans—the will is caught between reason and the concupiscible desires.[55]

## Chastity and Continence

The virtue of chastity does not have as an object to suppress desires and the pleasure of senses. Chastity is not achieved by removing passions, but rather, by participating in their activities in a way that is ordered and reasonable. In order for the virtue of temperance to be exercised not only is reason to be used, but the passions themselves so that the passions participate from within in a love that is reasonable. Because of the union between body and soul, matter and spirit in the person, it is in the nature of the passions to seek reason for moderation.[56] As I noted in chapter 3 with virtues, passions move beyond the principle of pleasure ascending towards moral beauty in which they participate.[57] A truly chaste person will love their spirit and their passions, and the moral beauty of chastity.

Continence is a step towards the virtue of chastity, it is not a perfect virtue in itself since the complete integration of inferior and superior powers is not present nor is there order in the sexual passions. In the case of the sexual addict, the order of reason is completely reversed where reason is completely submitted to sexual passions, while in the case of the continent person, the sexual passions are ordered, and reason succumbs to them.[58] It is during the phase that the addict is said not to be acting out over a given period of time, such as two months, that "continence" applies; once these choices have been integrated where the superior powers dominate, then, the individual may be said to be chaste. Since virtues are interconnected, one cannot just speak of one virtue existing on its own, but rather, each virtue is acquired with another—

55. Rom 7:14–24.
56. *ST* 2–2–151.1, *resp, ad* 1.
57. *ST* 2–2–145.3, *resp.*
58. *ST* 2–2–155.3, *resp.*

to have temperance means that force, prudence and justice are also needed. I discussed temperance above, but along with temperance is force, that is, a deliberate choice to limiting or reducing one's sexual acts as a path to abstinence. In this regard it is continence rather than being chaste, since chastity is integrated with the body and is acquired over time. Similarly, an addict comes to recognize that there is a lack of justice towards his-/her own body and/or that of others, where the body has become instrumentalized for purposes of sexual pleasure and gratification. The role of prudence is to help the individual examine the situation, and make choices according to the ultimate end, rather than a momentary good.[59]

As the sexual addict becomes temperate with the aim of being chaste, as I indicated above, first of all through the gratuitous relationship with a spiritual counselor, the counselor seeks the authentic good of the addict. From this first encounter, other relationships can be rediscovered with friends and family that may have been abandoned, and then opening up to new relationships. Moving from either the isolated sexual experiences of pornography and masturbation to creative non-sexual outlets, and to other experiences of pleasure that are relational, but re-ordered without sexual objectives, the recovering addict discovers the gratuity of friendship. Sexual addicts can all benefit from group meetings where they share their personal stories, weaknesses as well as their hopes, so they do not feel alone which further creates feelings of alienation and rejection. The possibility of group projects or activities by doing volunteer work for different communities, are amongst the possibilities.

The Sacramental life is where the person receives the graces needed to overcome weaknesses of the ongoing battle with sexual images, sexual encounters, and with seeking sexual gratification. Graces are received through the Holy Eucharist, Reconciliation and prayer. Both Sacraments serve to spiritually purify the person, to re-integrate them as complete beings from fragmentation to unity, but also to give the person a new start, a new beginning from the previous acting out to one of abstinence, and deepening a

59. *ST* 2–2–47.1, *ad* 2.

greater desire to be chaste. Moreover, the Eucharist and Reconciliation support and nurture the reintegration of the sexual addict in a faith community where relationships can be fostered and flourish, and where the person also experiences communion with God.

## Eschaton

Christ emerged out of a religion that expressed a high regard for the sexual life because of procreation which was seen as a blessing. However, Christ, from the very example of his unmarried state, showed the value of the celibate life, a radical departure from his own cultural norms. St. Paul's teachings showed that abstinence not only had an ascetic value, but also, and more importantly, were of eschatological significance.[60] Human sexuality in the Christian tradition cannot be separated from this eschatological vision where abstinence and chasteness serve the powerful end of union with God as the eschaton of reality. The absence of sexuality in the afterlife is similar to the absence of any form of vegetative life—it is not a denial of what God created, but the reality of a theocentric finality on earth and in paradise. Since the vegetative/sensory appetites are those that are shared with animals, the afterlife will be expressed in what is specifically shared with the divine, the spiritual appetite, the domain of the intelligence and the will.

Chastity as a religious virtue which Christians are called to live, has as its foundation in hope and charity. Hope is not just that things may change for the better here and now, but for eternal life. Chastity is not an exercise in stoic asceticism for personal self-growth or communal living. But rather, chastity is ordering one's life to another reality that transcends space and time as we know it, "As it was by one man that death came, so through one man has come the resurrection of the dead."[61] The original state of a person, that is, Adam's state, is not the result of the force of his nature, but

60. 1 Cor 7:29–31.

61. 1 Cor 15:19–23.

the result of the grace of original justice.[62] Christian chastity is motivated by the truths of faith which gives a different way of looking at sexual passion; the body is under the motion of the Holy Spirit and with this, a new and supernatural life as St. Paul states in Galatians, "All who belong to Christ Jesus have crucified self with all its passions and its desires. Since we are living by the Spirit, let our behavior be guided by the Spirit."[63] St. Paul's letters place human sexuality of the Christian at another level, at a supernatural one.

Associated with this virtue of hope is faith in Jesus Christ who will transform the mortal human body into incorruptible ones. This future anticipation gives sense to the virtue of chastity. This is what it means to hope as far as the future glory is concerned. All the theological virtues that grace gives to the individual are exercised in chastity: the virtue of chastity is sanctifying as far as it raises the order of reason to the supernatural order.[64] The only way to achieve a healthy sexuality is through an integrated morality, spiritual and sexual, emotional and affective. An authentic morality that faith teaches the individual is based on love and liberty, and the dynamism of interior truth.[65] This is what the Gospel teaches, this is what Christ taught. The return to God is possible because the human creature is a rational creature, created in God's image, and by reasonable acts based on virtue, with the help of grace, we can return to the Creator.

The individual believer, grows, ascends, descends, collapses, rises again, and so forth. The exterior laws help the interior conversion and may help the believing Christian at different stages when vulnerability is present whether this is due to loneliness or temptation. A mature Christian can still fall into serious sin, and by God's grace needs help to rise once again. The freedom the individual has to return to the Creator is by faith that operates through charity, and this is made possible by that grace of the Holy Spirit operating in the individual.[66]

62. *ST* 1–100.1, *resp.*

63. Gal 5:24–25.

64. Plé, *Vie Affective*, 174.

65. Plé, *Vie Affective*, 175.

66. *ST* 1–2–108.1, *resp.*

# Conclusion

This work has explored the problem of sexual addiction with a threefold objective: first, to consider the signs and causes of sexual addiction; second, to offer a moral evaluation for sexual addiction in its different manifestations; and third, on the basis of the moral reflection, to consider spiritual/pastoral paths of guidance and care for the persons struggling with sexual addiction, and seeking help.

How can we offer an adequate moral evaluation of someone who acknowledges that their sexual behavior is out of control, and manifests serious difficulties ordering their sexual life. It would appear that sexual addicts cannot be simply regarded as individuals who lead a "promiscuous" sexual lifestyle, as if this were their deliberate choice. The Christian response from a Thomistic framework that I have presented together with references to clinical studies, psychoanalysis and neurobiology, provide elements for a moral evaluation and some paths of support, to help the person with sexual addiction towards recovery by emphasizing virtue, grace and the Sacramental life.

In the first part of my work I focused on giving a description of sexual addiction by considering the different signs, and the associated causes. I considered ten signs of sexual addiction which included causal interpretations, and I subsumed these signs into three categories of identifiable behavior patterns, "repeated sexual acts," "out-of-control behavior" and "severe consequences." In my work I considered the psychoanalytical interpretations of sexual addiction to take into account unconscious or underlying factors for an addict's sexually compulsive tendencies. I further considered findings in neurobiology. I looked specifically at four types of addiction which are interconnected: pornography, masturbation, cybersex and multiple sexual partners. I explored in particular these addictions as possible ego-defense mechanisms manifesting some kind of underlying neurotic condition due to early stages of psychosexual development, sexual abuse, precocious sexual experiences or even "shame."

After an examination of sexual addiction, I proceeded with a moral anthropology based on St. Thomas Aquinas. The Thomistic anthropology looked at human nature and the human faculties, as well as internal principles such as virtue, and external principles such as law and grace, as a basis of constructing a moral foundation to examine sexual addiction. In this anthropology, human nature has a central role to play, especially the relationship between reason and the will. A further consideration was the "morality" of pleasure. I also examined the moral implications of "lust" as presented by Aquinas.

After the moral anthropology that is developed, I proceeded with a moral assessment of sexual addiction and paths of support. Drawing from the Thomistic anthropology the moral evaluation looked at the previous four addictions studied, pornography, masturbation, cybersex and multiple sexual partners. Finally, I considered avenues of both psychological and spiritual/pastoral support for the sexual addict as a means of offering guidance towards abstinence and chastity. This gradual recovery from sexual addiction with the suggested care is considered in the light of the Christian eschaton.

# Bibliography

American Society of Addiction Medicine. "Definition of Addiction." April 12, 2011.

Aquinas, Thomas. *Summa Theologiae*. Translated by the English Dominican Fathers. London: Burns, Oates & Washbourne, 1920.

Ariely, D., and G. Loewenstein. "The Heat of the Moment: The Effect of Sexual Arousal on Sexual Decision-Making." *Journal of Behavioral Decision Making* 19/2 (2006) 87–98.

Aristotle. *The Basic Works of Aristotle*. Edited by Richard McKeon. New York: Modern Library, 2001.

Augustine. *Confessions*. Translated by William Watts. Cambridge, MA: Harvard University Press, 2000.

———. *De Libero Arbitrio*. Translated by Anna S. Benjamin and L. H. Hackstaff. Upper Saddle River, NJ: Prentice Hall, 1964.

Bellusci, David C. *Amor Dei in the Sixteenth and Seventeenth Centuries*. Amsterdam: Rodopi, 2013.

———. "Christian Morality: Pelagius and St. Augustine." *Maritain Studies* 27 (2011) 67–82.

———. "Treating Sexual Addiction: Classical Schools of Psychotherapy of Freud, Frankl and Maslow." *Foundation Theology* (2017) 1–16.

Bernstein, A. "Beyond Counter Transference: The Love that Cures." *Modern Psychoanalysis* 26/2 (2001) 249–56.

———. "The Female Oedipal Complex." In *The Personal Myth in Psycho-Analytic Theory*, edited by P. Hartocollis and I. D. Graham, 183–219. Madison, CT: International Universities Press, 1991.

Berridge, K. C., and P. Winkielman. "What Is an Unconscious Emotion? (The Case for Unconscious 'Liking')." *Cognition and Emotion* 17/2 (2003) 181–211.

Black, D. W. "The Epidemiology and Phenomenology of Compulsive Sexual Behavior." *CNS Spectrums* 5 (2000) 26–72.

Black, Donald W., et al. "Characteristics of 36 Subjects Reporting Compulsive Sexual Behavior." *American Journal of Psychiatry* 154 (1997) 243–49.

# Bibliography

Bradshaw, John. "Cybersex, Courtship and Escalating Arousal: Factors in Addictive Sexual Desire." *Sexual Addiction and Compulsivity* 8/1 (2001) 45–78.

————. *Healing the Shame that Binds You*. Deerfield Beach, FL: Health Communications, 2005.

Carnes, Patrick. "Cybersex, Courtship, and Escalating Arousal: Factors in Addictive Sexual Desire." *Sexual Addiction and Compulsivity* 8/1 (2001) 45–78.

————. *Don't Call It Love*. New York: Bantam, 1991.

Cooper, Al. "Sexuality and the Internet: Surfing into a New Millennium." *Cyberpsychology and Behavior* 1/2 (1998) 187–93.

Cooper, Al, et al. "Online Sexual Activity: An Examination of Potentially Problematic Behaviors." *Sexual Addiction and Compulsivity* 11/3 (2004) 129–43.

Cucci, Giovanni. *Dipendenza Sessuale Online*. Milan: Ancora, 2015.

Delmonico, David, et al. "Treating Online Compulsive Sexual Behavior: When Cybersex Is the Drug of Choice." In *Sex and the Internet*, edited by Al Cooper, 147–67. New York: Brunner-Routledge, 2002.

De Saussure, Ferdinand. "Metapsychologie du Plaisir." *Revue Française de Psychanalyse* (1958) 649–74.

Dozois, David J. A., and Philip Firestone. *Abnormal Psychology*. 4th ed. Toronto: Prentice Hall, 2010.

Engler, Barbara. *Personality Theories*. New York: Houghton Mifflin, 2008.

Erdelyi, M. H. "Defense Processes Can Be Conscious or Unconscious." *American Psychologist* 56/9 (2001) 761–63.

Erikson, Erik. *Childhood and Society*. London: Vintage, 1995.

Farley, Margaret A. *A Framework for Christian Sexual Ethics*. New York: Continuum, 2008.

Finkelhor, D., et al. *Online Victimization: A Report on the Nation's Youth*. Alexandria, VA: National Center for Missing and Exploited Children, 2000.

Finnis, John M. "Law, Morality, and 'Sexual Orientation.'" *Notre Dame Law Review* 69 (1994) 1049–76.

Freud, Sigmund. *Civilizations and Its Discontents*. Translated by Joan Riviere. Mansfield: Martino, 2010.

————. "Formulations Regarding the Two Principles in Mental Functioning." In *Organization and Pathology of Thought: Selected Sources*, edited by David Rapaport, 315–28. New York: Columbia University Press, 1951.

————. "Pour Introduire au Narcissisme." In *La Vie Sexuelle*, translated by Denise Berger et al., 81–105. Introduction by Jean Laplace. Paris: Presses Universitaires de France, 1985.

Garrett, Richard. "Addiction, Paradox, and the Good I Would." In *Addiction and Responsibility*, edited by Poland and Graham, 247–68, Cambridge, MA: MIT, 2011.

# Bibliography

Goldberg, Barbara. "Social Working Leads to Sex Faster?" *Reuters*, January 25, 2011.

Greenfield, Patricia. "Inadvertent Exposure to Pornography on the Internet: Implications of Peer-to-Peer File-Sharing Networks for Child Development and Families." *Applied Development Psychology* 25 (2004) 741–50.

Grizer, Germain. *The Way of the Lord Jesus.* Vol. 2, *Christian Living.* Quincy, IL: Franciscan, 1993.

Grünbaum, A. *Validation in the Clinical Theory of Psychoanalysis.* New York: International Universities Press, 1993.

Guerreschi, C. *La Dipendenza Sessuale. Quando il Sesso Può Uccidere.* Cinisello Balsamo: San Paolo, 2005.

Harris, Richard Jackson. *A Cognitive Psychology of Mass Communication.* New York: Routledge, 2009.

Kafka, Martin. "Hypersexual Desire Disorder in Males: An Operational Definition and Clinical Implications for Males with *Paraphilias* and *Paraphilia*-related Disorders." *Archives of Sexual Behaviors* 26 (1997) 505–26.

———. "Hypersexual Disorder: A Proposed Diagnosis for DSM-V." *Archives of Sexual Behavior* 39 (2000) 377–400.

J. Laplanche, and J.-B. Pontalis. *Vocabulaire de la Psychanalyse.* Paris: Presses Universitaires de France, 1967.

Layden, Mary Anne. "Testimony for U.S Senate Committee on Commerce, Science and Transportation." Center for Cognitive Therapy, Department of Psychiatry, University of Pennsylvania. November 18, 2004.

Longo, Robert, et al. "Effects of Internet Sexuality on Children and Adolescents." In *Sex and the Internet: A Guidebook for Clinicians,* edited by A. Cooper, 87–105. New York: Brunner-Routledge, 2002.

MacKinnon, Catharine A., and Andrea Dworkin, eds. *In Harm's Way: The Pornography Civil Rights Hearings.* Cambridge, MA: Harvard University Press, 1997.

McIlhaney, Joe S., and Freda McKissic Bush. *Hooked: New Science on How Casual Sex Is Affecting Our Children.* Chicago: Northfield, 2008.

Melis, M. R., and A. Agriolas. "Dopamine and Sexual Behaviour." *Neuroscience and Biobehavioral Reviews* 19/1 (1995) 19–38.

Milkman, Harvey, and Stanley Sunderwirth. *Craving for Ecstasy: The Consciousness of Chemistry and Escape.* Lexington, MA: Lexington, 1986.

Pellai, A. "La Cittinanza Intima." *Psicologia Contemporanea* 243 (2014) 24–29.

Pinckaers, Servais. *The Sources of Christian Ethics.* Translated by Mary Thomas Noble. Washington, DC: Catholic University of America Press, 1995.

Plato. *The Collected Dialogues of Plato.* Edited by Edith Hamilton and Huntington Cairns. Princeton: Princeton University Press, 1999.

Plé, Albert. *Par Pouvoir ou Par Plaisir?* Paris: Cerf, 1980.

———. *Vie Affective et Chasteté.* Paris: Cerf, 1964.

Poland, Jeffrey, and George Graham, eds. *Addiction and Responsibility.* Cambridge, MA: MIT Press, 2011.

# Bibliography

Porter, Jean. *Natural and Divine Law*. Ottawa: Novalis, 1999.

Rahey, John R., and Erick Hagerman. *Spark, the Revolutionary New Science of Exercise and the Brain*. New York: Little Brown, 2008.

Richards, A. D. "The Future of Psychoanalysis: The Past, Present, and Future of Psychoanalytic Theory." *Psychoanalytic Quarterly* 59 (1990) 347–69.

Schneider, J. P. "Effects of Cybersex Problems on the Spouse and Family." In *Sex and the Internet: A Guidebook for Clinicians*, edited by A. Cooper, 169–86. New York: Brunner-Routledge, 2002.

Silverman, Sue. *Love Sick*. New York: Norton, 2001.

Small, F. E. "The Psychology of Women: A Psychoanalytic Review." *Canadian Journal of Psychiatry* 34/9 (1989) 872–78.

Stack, Steven, et al. "Adult Social Bonds and Use of Internet Pornography." *Social Science Quarterly* 85 (2004) 75–88.

Stein, Dan J., et al. "Hypersexual Disorder and Preoccupation with Internet Pornography." *American Journal of Psychiatry* 158/10 (2010) 1590–94.

Struthers, William M. *Wired for Intimacy: How Pornography Hijacks the Male Brain*. Madison, WI: InterVarsity, 2009.

Thevenot, Xavier. *Repères Éthiques*. Mulhouse: Salvator, 1983.

Vergote, Antoine. *"Tu aimeras le Seigneur Ton Dieu . . ."* Paris: Cerf, 1997.

Vogt, Emmerich. *The Freedom to Love*. Minneapolis: Mill City, 2012.

Weaver, James B., III. "The Effects of Pornography Addiction on Families and Communities." Testimony presented before the Subcommittee on Science, Technology, and Space of the Senate Committee on Commerce, Science, and Transportation. Washington, DC, November 18, 2004.

Young, Kimberly. *Caught in the Net*. New York: Wiley, 1998.

Züllmann, Dolf, and Jennings Bryant. "Pornography's Impact on Sexual Satisfaction." *Journal of Applied Social Psychology* 18 (1988) 438–53.

# Index

# Index

Carnes, Patrick, 2n.6, 3, 96
castration anxiety, 94–95
*Catechism of the Catholic Church,*
 26
change of mood, sexual addiction
 and, 9
chastity, 109–11
children, precocious sexual patterns in, 8
circumstance, of pleasure, 73
Commandments of God, 82–85
compulsive behavior, masturbation as, 29–30
concupiscence, 42–43
 passion and, 47–50
 sin and, 61
conflictual elements
 in sexual addiction, 94–98
 in sexuality, 94–95
conscience, sexual addiction and,
 3, 7
consent
 basis of, 74
 to sin, 81–82
continence, 109–11
Convention Relating to Certain,
 15
conversion therapy, sexual addiction and, 104–6
craving, 72–73
creation, sexuality and, 76–77
Cucci, Giovanni, 3n.13, 11, 89
cybersex, 27–28, 30–32, 90–92

Declaration 53, 278
defense mechanisms, 23–25
*delectatio,* Aquinas's concept of,
 70–71
delight, 48–49
denial, 24–25
Diagnostic and Statistical Manual
 of Mental Disorders (DSM),
 24–25
disposition, habit and, 51–53
divine grace, 65–66

divine order, sexuality and, 76–77
dopamine, 20–21

ego, 19–20
ego-defense mechanisms, 23–25
emotional culpability, 21–23
end, Aquinas's discussion of,
 62–64
Erikson, Erik, 21–22
eschaton, 111–12
external principles, 61–67
 end and finality, 62–64
 sexuality and, 96–98
extrinsic principles
 imagination and, 50–51
 passions and, 46–50
 will and, 45–46
Eye Movement Desensitization
 Reprocessing (EMDR)
 therapy, 100

faculties, human nature and,
 39–51
fall, consequences of, 80–81
family environment
 multiple sexual partners and,
 32–33
 sexual addiction and, 108–9
 sexuality and, 11, 96–98
finality, Aquinas's discussion of,
 62–64
freedom
 Aquinas on, 34, 61–62
 grace and, 66
 love and, 67
 natural law and, 41–42
 obedience and, 65
 pleasure and, 68–72
 sexuality and, 28
 Thomist perspective on, 41–42
Freudian psychoanalysis, sexual
 addiction and, 15–20, 93, 98,
 101–2
*fruitio,* 49

# Index

# Index